What parents and educators are saying about
Teaching Children Joy:

"If you want happy children, read this book!"

> —Jane Wolsey
> Lethbridge, Alberta, Canada

"It is about time we learn about positive parenting skills. I'm pleased to see experienced parents sharing their positive ideas and methods for teaching children the joys of life, before problems occur. This positive thrust—acting rather than reacting—can be a valuable parenting tool."

> —Catherine C. Peterson
> 1983 National Young Mother
> Orfield, Pennsylvania

"Most parents, including myself, need more than theories, more than books full of good ideas and techniques. We need an ongoing program *that puts us together with other parents monthly and gives us objectives, incentives, and a track to run on. This is what* Teaching Children Joy *does."*

> —Carol Kenley
> Palmer, Alaska

"Our entire family has long followed those philosophies that make the family unit more unified, more organized, and more in harmony with each other's personalities and needs. This volume by the Eyres reinforces those philosophies and concepts in such a way that it serves as a road map to all active and progressive parents seeking day-to-day enrichment and counsel. It is a much-needed book for our time."

> —Merrill Osmond
> Singer, producer, composer
> Provo, Utah

Teaching Children Joy

Teaching Children Joy
Linda and Richard Eyre

SHADOW MOUNTAIN

Salt Lake City, Utah

Shadow Mountain is an imprint of Deseret Book Company,
P.O. Box 30178, Salt Lake City, Utah 84130.

Contents

Preface to the Second Edition

In 1980, the first edition of *Teaching Children Joy* was published in a limited, regional edition as a guide for the parents of pre-school-age children. That first edition went through multiple printings and became the basis for thousands of "TCJ parents' groups,"* in which parents form cooperative neighborhood "Joy Schools" in their homes, rotating as teachers.

Because of the positive responses from parents and TCJ members we are especially pleased, through this special national edition, to make *Teaching Children Joy* broadly available to parents throughout the country.

We wrote this book and started the TCJ parent group system because of our strong disagreement with the common supposition that the greatest thing a child can possess (or that parents can help him attain so he can "succeed" in today's society) is a high I.Q. Too much stress is placed on young children's abilities, on their being able to put together numbers and letters quickly, on manipulation skills. The world at large seems to be overly aware of "How soon will my child read?" or "Just listen to him count (or recite)." While such things do have their place, we strongly believe that real happiness, contentment, and ability to cope with the world lie in a child's J.Q. (joy quotient). Ponder, for a moment, the quality of a child's life once he has obtained confidence in his own ability to make decisions, to enjoy and be aware of nature, to understand another person's feelings, to set a goal and accomplish it, to share with and serve his friends, and to see himself as a unique

---

*See postscript at end of book for more information about TCJ parent groups.

individual with a great deal to offer to others. Each of these are *joys* that can be taught, and we are of the opinion that the ideal time to teach them is before the age of five and before the beginning of formal education. To a child who has a foundation of these "joy" concepts, the other abilities often associated with I.Q. will come quickly and naturally. By teaching a child joy, we can give him both an active mind and an attitude and legacy of happiness.

The current trend toward a renewal of strong family commitments is not based on some new sense of obligation or responsibility. It is based on the rediscovery that children are fun, that families are a source of joy, that the rest of life supports the family and not vice versa. Bookstores are filled with books on the joy of cooking, the joy of jogging, the joy of gardening, the joy of meditation; but the most genuine lasting joy is the joy of families.

Acknowledgments

This is essentially a method book. Each chapter is a list of methods for teaching a particular type of joy to small children. Many of the methods evolved from two sources, each of which merits strong acknowledgment at the beginning of this book. 1. The experimental Joy School started in 1974 in Logan, Utah. Mrs. Ruth Eyre, who possesses exceptional gifts in understanding, teaching, and motivating small children (and who is also our mother), was and continues to be the head teacher there and the developer and perfector of many of the ideas for *Teaching Children Joy*. 2. The tens of thousands of members of TCJ, a national parenting co-op. Each member is part of a neighborhood "do-it-yourself" Joy School where members rotate as teachers of groups of preschoolers. Mrs. Corry DeMille and her staff have carefully managed this nationwide network of families and have given us feedback and ideas from hundreds of interested and capable parents.

Introduction: To You as a Parent

There are in my memory some small, bright, open places that never close or fade. I remember as if it were yesterday the moment when the doctor put our just-delivered, still-wet, first child on my trembling arm.

I remember the outside things: the antiseptic hospital smell, the combination of joy and fatigue on my wife's face, the exquisite perfection of each tiny new finger and toe. Even more, I remember the inside feelings: the sighing relief, the welling joy, the almost irrestible urge to throw open the hospital window right then (at 3:00 A.M.) and announce the new arrival to the world.

Just under the joy was another feeling: the weight of responsibility, the sudden remarkable reality that this tiny, real person was ours now, ours to raise, her destiny so totally entrusted to our inexperienced, untried, untrained parenthood.

Within the next hour there were calls to new grandparents and the fun of hearing their voices jump from grogginess to excitement. Then, finally, with new baby and new mother fast asleep, there was nothing more for me to do but drive home. By then it was early-summer dawn, with deserted streets and delicate, pale gold sky. Spontaneously, as I drove, I felt a deeper joy and gratitude than I had ever known.

I also felt, simultaneously, the strongest desire I had ever felt: the desire to do well, to succeed as a parent. I promised myself that somehow I would.

Nearly two years later, our second child was born. Maybe you've felt what we experienced at that time: the concern that comes from *being* parents before having learned *how* to be parents.

1

We could already see how different this second child was from the first, and the frightful thought occurred that all our hard-learned, trial-and-error lessons on how to handle the first wouldn't work at all on the second. We realized we were beginner parents in an advanced class. We had gone to school for fifteen or twenty years to learn the concepts and skills necessary for our professions, but we didn't have a single credit-hour toward parenting.

Because I had just emerged from graduate school, I took a student's approach to parenting. I responded to my fears by going to the nearest bookstore, where I bought eleven paperback books on parenting. Back at home, I spread them out on the table and began to study. My idea was to speed-read them all, to find areas of consensus. If several experts agreed on something, it had to be right.

What a shock to discover that none of them agreed on anything! Just when I had been convinced of one author's view on discipline, another author argued so compellingly for an opposite theory that I changed my mind. The writers' credentials and degrees didn't lead them to similar views at all, but simply gave them license to disagree very convincingly. It also concerned me, as I read their credentials, that many of them were not even parents. They were psychiatrists who had learned on other people's children!

We responded to their disagreements by throwing all the books away and adopting still another approach. We decided to disregard all "expertise" and adopt the simplest view of all: namely, that techniques and theories don't even matter—that the whole key is *love*. We would simply love our children with all our hearts, and everything else would take care of itself.

That notion lasted only until we realized how much evidence there was against it. My business partner and his wife, we observed, loved their daughter and showed it by giving her everything she wanted. The result of their love was an insufferably spoiled and unhappy child. A neighbor of ours loved his son and showed it by spending every spare moment trying to make him into the ball player he had always wanted his son to be. The result of his love was a nervous, erratic child who was making neither himself nor his father happy.

It occurred to us that love must be intelligent rather than indulgent, that love applied unintelligently can be harmful.

We realized once again that we needed at least a basic philosophy for parenting, a set of parental goals and some notions of how to achieve them, a framework within which to apply our love.

We realized that the real problem with the eleven parenting books was that they were not based on *objectives*, on any positive, specific notions of what parents should be trying to *give* their children. Instead, they were based on reacting rather than acting. Their tone was, "If Johnny does this, you try this." They were a defense rather than an offense.

So we began to search for objectives. We began to ask what we most wanted for our children, what we wanted to give them. It seemed like the right question. We would simply base our parenting on what we wanted to give our children. The trouble was, there were so many things: security, confidence, creativity, friendliness, peace of mind, self-esteem, imagination, concern for others, individuality, a sense of service. The list kept getting longer. What we were developing was a wish list rather than a workable philosophy.

The breakthrough occurred one evening when we had the opportunity to speak to a large group of parents. We handed out a slip of paper to each couple and asked them to write the ages of their children on one side. On the other side they were to write, in one word, the thing they would most like to *give* their children. We said, "If you had a one-word wish for your children, what would it be?"

The results were quite remarkable. Virtually all parents of preschoolers said the same thing. Parents of elementary-school-age children were also relatively unified, but in a different direction. Parents of teenagers had still another wish. For preschoolers, parents wanted *happiness*. For elementary-school-age children, parents hoped for *responsibility*. And for teenagers, most parents wished for more unselfishness, more *service* and less self-centeredness.

We realized, as we tabulated the results, that most parents do know, at least in general terms, what their children need. They know what they would like to give them—they just do not always know *how* to give it. The challenge, we decided, was to break these objectives down, to simplify them, and to come up with practical methods through which parents could teach them to children.

It was the beginning of our program of "parenting by objective." We decided that we would consciously adopt the following objectives and sequence:

Ages 0-6: Teach our children *joy*.

Ages 4-12: Teach our children *responsibility*.

Ages 10-16: Teach our children *service* and *charity*.

We knew there were overlaps. There were elements of responsibility within joy, and service within responsibility, but we felt that we needed a focus—a clear, strong, single goal to work on for each phase of a child's growth.

This book, *Teaching Children Joy*, was born out of our efforts and those of thousands of other parents who eventually worked with us to "subdivide" *joy* and to develop simple methods (stories, games, songs, activities) through which each kind of joy could be taught to small children.

Thinking about Joy

Once the word *joy* came into our formula, everything else began to fit. Children teach us so many kinds of joy: spontaneity, living in the present, being totally interested in and often thrilled with life. But they must learn other joys: sharing, service, setting and achieving goals, searching and finding, planting and harvesting.

Can young children gain these varieties of joy? Can they actually experience them at a tender age? Yes! All true forms of joy are simple and pure. Children can feel them more easily, more naturally than adults.

As thoughts and ideas began to click, we developed two personal commitments: (1) to start a "Joy School" to teach what we hadn't found in other preschools, and (2) to write this book to say what we hadn't found in other books.

The first objective was a joy to accomplish. We bought a house and converted it (a wall torn out here, a sandpile put in there) into a nursery school. We formulated and classified our ideas as we repainted walls. We defined and dissected and analyzed the concept of joy as we landscaped the yard. We worked out joy-teaching, joy-experiencing methods as we brought in toys and play equipment.

By the time the school opened we had developed a curriculum of thirteen separate "joys," and we had found many other parents who shared our view that the word *joy* summarized what we most wanted our children to gain.

Among our thirteen joys were four that children are born with, forms of joy that we hoped the school would buttress and encourage, strengthen and preserve. The other nine were joys we felt children had to gain, capacities they did not inherently possess but that they could feel if given the opportunity. Our mother, Ruth Eyre, with extensive background and expertise in early childhood education, became the head teacher at the Joy School and, along with the other teachers, accepted the challenge of developing the methods and teaching techniques that would permit small children to experience all thirteen kinds of joy.

The thirteen joys now become the thirteen chapters of this book. In each of the book's four sections, there is one joy to *preserve* and either two or three to *teach*. For example, the mental joy of curiosity and interest—which children are born with—can, if it is encouraged and preserved, become the basic vehicle for learning the joy of imagination and creativity and the joy of setting and achieving goals. As a second example, in the social joys, if we can preserve a child's natural openness and candor, that inherent joy can become the cup into which we pour the learned joys of communication and relationships and of sharing and service.

Each chapter—each joy—is presented in five simple parts:

1. *Examples and description.* To clearly identify and isolate what the joy is, one "child example" and one "adult example" begin each chapter. In the "joys-to-preserve" chapters, the child example comes first, since we learn the joy from our children. In the "joys-to-teach" chapters, the adult example comes first, followed by a child example that demonstrates that small children can experience that particular joy.

2. *Methods.* Several methods are then suggested, each with the objective of helping the child to experience and identify the particular joy. These are not presented in exhaustive detail, but rather in simplified, abbreviated, outline form so that the parent can catch their essence and then apply them with his own special personality and interpretation. Virtually all of the methods listed can be used both individually in the home by parents and in group situations (parents' groups or Joy Schools). Methods particularly suited to groups are noted in the text by an asterisk (*).

3. *Family focal point.* Most parents, with the daily concerns of occupation and obligation, cannot make up lesson plans or

think consistently about multiple methods. They can, however, remember and implement one "family focal point" for
each joy. Each focal point is a simple family idea (a clear habit
or tradition or practice) that keeps that joy prominent and
conscious in the minds of family members.

4. *A story for parents to read to children,* one that illustrates
and dramatizes the joy.

5. *A reading list* of children's stories that are about "that
joy." While there may be scores of children's books that could
apply to each chapter, this is a selective, handpicked list of the
ones we consider to be the best.

In parts one and three of each chapter, we have been
somewhat personal because we felt that we could best describe
each "joy" by relating what we have felt in our own family. Our
eight children appear in the pages of the book at varying ages,
depending on when the incident we are describing took place.

Being a conscientious, involved parent of preschoolers can
be an exhausting proposition. But is does not have to be so.
Consider for a moment the statement of a well-known physi-
cian, Dr. Scott J. Wilson of Florida: "Those who are working
toward constructive, clearly defined goals hardly ever feel
fatigue."

The "bottom line" of parenting by objective is that as we ac-
tively pursue clear, worthwhile goals with our children, much
of the day-to-day frustration and weariness falls away.

One problem most parents face is a difficulty in measuring
their success. Since they do not have specific goals for a
"yardstick," they not only do more reacting than acting, they
end up measuring their success by the emotions of frustration
and impatience that they often feel.

A parent with one basic objective each month, on the other
hand, can look past the momentary crises that come to all
families and can see the progress the children are making in
the area of that monthly goal. This is why we recommend that
you select one "joy" to focus on each month. Use the methods
suggested in the book and add others of your own. You will
find that just your awareness of the month's joy will cause you
to find unplanned, spur-of-the-moment ways to teach it.

If, as you read, you try to think about all of the "joys" and
all of the methods for teaching them at once, you will feel
overwhelmed. If you focus only on one joy each month you
will feel comfortable and relaxed.

PHYSICAL JOYS

"Nature never makes haste. Her systems revolve at an even pace . . . the bud swells imperceptibly, without hurry or confusion, as though the short spring days were an eternity." (Henry David Thoreau.)

Thoreau's words could also describe a small child observing nature or learning to use and appreciate his body. Children are not in a hurry. The haste and hassle of the world have yet to overtake them. They can thus experience many physical forms of joy more intensely and meaningfully than can most adults, whose appreciation is dimmed by longer experience with the earth's wonders.

All the world is new to the child, and his own body is his most intriguing plaything. All is fresh and exciting.

With the right kind of instruction and encouragement from their parents, preschool children can draw from everyday life vast quantities of physical joy. They can thrill at the world around them and the ability of their senses to receive its joy. Their natural, spontaneous delight can be preserved and intensified and even made contageous so that their parent-teachers begin to reexperience a more acute sense of physical joy.

Preserving the Joy of Spontaneous Delight

1

"The world will never starve for want of wonders." (G. K. Chesterton.)

I. Examples and Description

A. *Child:* I was upstairs in my bedroom; eighteen-month-old Josh was right below me downstairs in his sister's room. At first I thought he was crying, but as I listened again, I heard it for what it was: a loud, spontaneous belly-laugh. I knew he was down there by himself, because I could hear his sisters with Linda in the kitchen, so I sneaked quietly down to observe. I peeked through the door just in time for the next peal of laughter. Josh, his back to me, was sitting on his haunches facing Saren's bed. The bedspread, hanging to the floor, suddenly bulged and then lifted to reveal Barney, our big black Labrador, squirming out from under the bed. There was something funny about Barney's shifty-eyed, sheepish look as he pushed his head out from under the spread. Josh laughed so hard he fell sideways. Then he promptly crawled under the end of the bed (Barney following), crawled back out from under the bedspread, and turned to watch Barney come out again.

Josh's laugh made me smile, made me feel free. Adult laughter is too often sarcastic or boisterous or somehow forced and brittle. Josh's spontaneous laugh pealed out like a thousand bells—the kind of free, delighted laugh that most little children have and most adults lose.

There is often a paradox in adult minds. On one hand, we admire spontaneity; we speak of the free spirit, the unconventional, with at least a lingering trickle of envy. On the other hand, we associate maturity with words like *sophistication, reserve,* and *proper.* Too often parents convey the inhibitions of "the other hand" to their children. How many times have you seen a parent give a sideward, brow-furrowed look of scorn to a child whose spontaneous delight and enthusiasm were "socially improper"? We let our own inferiorities and inhibitions stamp out the spontaneity in our children, and we let our schools and institutions do the same thing. If we are not careful, it becomes harder to preserve and protect in our children the joys they were born with than to teach them new ones.

B. *Adult:* I was alone one day, walking to lunch on a busy Boston street. Ahead was an old man, begging, "Any spare change?" The young businessman ahead of me brushed him off. "No, no—sorry." Too busy. Life is a pattern, each man with an image of himself. The businessman was sophisticated, on a time schedule: "can't be interrupted," "don't stop for this unsavory character," "he's not on my daily calendar." Then I came up to the beggar. I saw his face. I saw character mixed with tragedy in the old eyes. "Come on—come to lunch with me." Spontaneous, spur of the moment. The man was surprised. I was surprised. I'll forget other lunches, but never that one. The incredible story of a broken man's life—it did him good to tell it; it did me good to hear it. He left with a full stomach and with a flicker of hope because someone had cared and listened. I left happy because I had helped, but also because I had done something spontaneous—free—open.

II. Methods

As with each of the "joys to preserve," the key method is encouragement and reinforcement. Children will repeat what they are praised for.

There are many ways to encourage and sanction a particular behavior; perhaps the best way of all is by participating in that particular behavior yourself. (And perhaps the great benefit of preserving the natural, childlike joys in children is that we may recapture them in ourselves.)

A. *Get excited with children.* Swallow your sophistication— be a child with them, emote with them. When they say, "Oh, look!" you say, "Wow, yes!" Don't say, "Calm down, son," or "Not here, dear." Let them be your teachers. They are the experts in spontaneity—do what they do. Live in the present with them. Praise them for watching, and watch with them what they watch!

B. *Help them relive spontaneous joy moments by remembering.* "Remember when we saw the bird pulling up the worm, Saydi? Wasn't that great?" "Remember at the picnic when the grasshopper jumped into the potato salad? Didn't we laugh hard?"

C. *Do spontaneous things with them.* "Hey, Shawni, instead of a bedtime story tonight, let's put on your pajamas and go to the ice cream shop for a cone before you go to bed." "Josh, your mom looks tired. Let's put *her* to bed for a nap, and you and I will fix dinner."

D. *Make spontaneity a high priority.* Place enough value on spontaneity that you let it happen even if it's a little inconvenient. Suppose you are walking outside on a warm summer afternoon and you spot your two-year-old stomping with delight in his first puddle. Resist the urge to yank him out with a "No, no!" Take off his shoes and let him do it. (Or take off *your* shoes and do it with him!)

E. *Play surprise-oriented group games.* Play games together in which the adults share and encourage the children's spontaneous delight, such as hide-and-seek and musical chairs.

F. *Open packages.* Wrap things up—share the surprise as children open them. Have them guess what's inside before opening.

G. *Put new surprises into old fairy tales.* It's amazing what delight the mixing of two familiar fairy tales can cause. "While the three bears were walking in the woods, they heard a funny little man singing a song: 'They'll never guess that Rumpelstiltskin is my name.'"

H. *Do things with children that are a little silly and that show how acceptable it is to enjoy unexpected things.*

1. Put a mitten on the doorknob and "shake hands" with the door.

2. Get up and do a little dance when the music and the mood hit you.

3. Catch grasshoppers in a field (in a delighted way).

*I. *Engage in the kind of play that produces exciting and unpredictable results.*

1. Blow bubbles with a straw (in a glass of soapy water, or in the tub at bath time).

2. Finger paint with thick paint. Let the children mix colors. Let them try it with their feet.

3. Play in water with empty plastic bottles, straws, or funnels.

*J. *Finger paint with shaving cream.* Squirt a small amount of aerosol shaving cream on a smooth formica surface or table in front of each child and sprinkle on a little red powdered tempera paint. Let the children spread it around with their fingers or whole hands. Then sprinkle on a little blue and yellow tempera paint in different places so they can mix colors and see what happens.

*K. *Pop popcorn without a lid.* Spread a sheet on the floor

---

*Asterisks indicate activities that work especially well in group situations.

and put a popcorn popper in the center of the sheet. Have the children sit around the edges. Put oil and corn in the popper and leave the lid on until it begins popping. You could sing songs or have a discussion while waiting. Ask the children, "What do you think will happen if I take off the lid?" Instruct them not to touch the hot kernels of popped corn. Then remove the lid and let the corn pop out. Don't inhibit the children's squealing and laughter more than necessary. (Hot air poppers also work if you can take off the top to let the popped corn fly.)

*L. *"Duck, Duck, Goose."* To play this game, you need enough room for the children to run around safely. It can be played inside or out. Children sit in a circle. One is "it." He goes around the circle touching each on the head and saying, "Duck, duck, duck," as he touches heads. Then he calls someone a "goose" as he touches that person's head. The "goose" must get up and chase him around the circle, trying to catch him before he slips into the "goose's" spot in the circle. Then the "goose" becomes "it" and the game is repeated.

*M. *Discussion.* Talk about how fun it is to sometimes do or say silly things, to surprise someone or have someone surprise you, to laugh and giggle. Tell the children they are better at this than you are because sometimes grownups forget how to be silly.

Think of a personal experience from your childhood when you experienced something funny or silly. Tell the children about it. Then let each child tell about something that makes him laugh or giggle.

*N. *Blowing bubbles.* Prepare a nontransparent container of water with a small amount of dishwashing liquid in it. Put a straw in the solution and say, "Did you ever do this?" Blow into the solution while the children listen and watch. When the bubbles are up over the top, raise the end of the straw up into the bubbles and blow slowly to make a *big* bubble. Appreciate their spontaneous delight and then let them try it.

*O. *Surprise box.* With the children on a sofa or the floor, show them a box with a lid labeled "surprises." Tell them what it says, and say, "Do you like surprises?" Peek in the box, act surprised, and take out one surprise at a time to "discover" with them. Suggested surprises are listed below. You may think of other good ideas.

1. A small box labeled "Yummy, yummy," containing one tiny marshmallow for each child.

2. A 35mm film can labeled "big or little." In it are stuffed two or three very sheer scarfs or handkerchiefs tied together at the corners. Pull them out slowly (practice ahead of time).

3. A "fake snake"—a cloth-covered spring wire in a can labeled "Nuts" or "Candy." This can be bought at a novelty shop. Stand back several feet from the children and open the can so the "snake" jumps out. Then let them feel it and know what it is. Do it again or let one of the children ask you, "Do you want some nuts?" and *you* be surprised when it jumps out on you.

4. A small toy mounted on a suction cup and spring (available at gift shops). You press it on a flat surface, and the suction cup gradually releases so the toy jumps at an unexpected moment. Have it in a small box labeled "Watch out." Take it out and press it on the palm of your hand. Let the children watch it jump.

III. Family Focal Point: The Family Treasure Chest

We have a "treasure chest." It is just an old wooden box, painted many beautiful colors, with a big combination lock on it. The children know from experience that there is always a surprise in it.

Once or twice a week, on special occasions or perhaps for rewards, the chest is opened by daddy, the only one who knows the lock's combination. It is amazing how delighted a child can be with one small piece of candy, a pinecone, or even a small sponge so he can help wipe off the table. Anything, so long as it comes out of the treasure chest, produces spontaneous delight.

IV. Story: "The Bears Save the Baby"

(This story is for children familiar with the stories of "The Three Bears" and "Rumpelstiltskin.")

Once upon a time there were three bears: a daddy bear, a mama bear, and a little baby bear. One day they were having soup for dinner, and the baby bear said, in his wee, little voice, "This soup is too hot."

"It is," said the daddy bear in his deep, big voice. "Let's go for a walk in the woods while it cools off."

So they did. They skipped off into the woods singing their

favorite song, which was "The Bear Went Over the Mountain." When the song ended and their voices were quiet, the baby bear said, "Shhh, listen—I hear someone else singing." They all listened, and they heard a little song coming out of the deepest part of the woods. "Let's go see who it is," said the mama bear. They crept very quietly, as only bears can do. Pretty soon they were close enough to hear the singer clearly. His was a strange, croaky little voice, and the song went like this:

> "Today I cook, tomorrow I bake,
> The next day the queen's child I take.
> For she will never, never proclaim
> That Rumpelstiltskin is my name."

The bears got close enough to see through the trees and into a little clearing. They saw a tiny, wicked-looking man dancing around his fire. He sang the last line again, "For Rumpelstiltskin is my name."

In a tiny whisper, the daddy bear said, "Come this way," and the three bears walked quickly and quietly away until they could not hear the little man anymore. Then the daddy bear said in his deep, big voice, "Who was that?"

"He was bad," said the baby bear in his high, squeaky voice.

"What was he singing about?" asked the mama bear in her soft, gentle voice.

Daddy: "About the little princess, I think."

Baby: "He is going to take her away from the queen."

Mama: "Unless the queen can guess his name."

Baby: "She'll never guess a funny name like Rumpelstiltskin."

Daddy: "Unless we tell her."

Baby: "Let's run to the palace."

Off went the three bears as fast as their legs would carry them. At last they saw the palace. At first the guard was afraid when he saw them, but the mama bear said in her soft, gentle voice, "Don't worry, we have come to tell the queen the name of the bad little elf."

"You know his name?" said the guard. "We've all been trying to figure it out. Come with me right this way."

When they found the queen, she was crying and sobbing. "How can I ever learn his name?"

"We know it, we know it," said the baby bear in his high, squeaky voice.

"What? Who are you?" asked the queen, looking up.

"We found the little man in the woods," said the big daddy bear respectfully. "He didn't see us but we heard him say his name."

The queen clapped her hands with joy, and the baby bear whispered in her ear, "Rumpelstiltskin."

That night when the little elf showed up, laughing and thinking that he would take the baby, the bears were carefully hidden under the table so they could watch.

"Well, you don't know my name," he said, "so I'll be taking the little princess."

"Let me guess first," said the queen. "You said I had three guesses."

"All right, but hurry," said the elf. "You can never guess it."

The queen was enjoying herself now. She decided to use all of her guesses before getting it right. "Is it Joshua?" she asked.

"No, no, no," laughed the little man, rubbing his hands together. "Guess again."

"Is it Jonah?" said the queen.

"No, no, no, no. You'll never guess."

"Well," said the queen, "for my last guess, is it Rumpelstiltskin?"

The elf turned red in the face with anger. He stomped his feet so hard that he disappeared right through the floor and was never seen again.

There was a great celebration at the palace, and the queen invited the bears to stay and to become special palace guards. The bears thanked her but said they had to get back to their house to see if their soup was cooled off yet.

V. Reading List (Including Out-of-print Titles)

Allard, H. *The Stupids Step Out.* Boston: Houghton Mifflin, 1974. (The Stupids do everything backward, up-side-down, etc.)

Asheron, S. *The Surprise in the Story Book.* New York: Grosset and Dunlap, 1963. (The anticipated discovery finally happens.)

Barrett, J. *Animals Should Definitely Not Wear Clothing*. New York: Atheneum, 1970. (Ridiculous pictures of the consequences.)

Baum, A. and J. *Know What? No, What?* New York: Parent's Magazine, 1964. (Nonsense riddles.)

Carle, E. *The Very Hungry Caterpillar*. New York: World Publishing Co., 1971. (A caterpillar eats right through the pages of the book.)

De Regniers, B. *What Can You Do with a Shoe?* New York: Harper & Row, 1955. (Silly, imaginative answers to riddles.)

Eastman, P. D. *Are You My Mother?* New York: Beginner Books, 1960. (A delightful story about a baby bird who is looking for his mother, whom he has never seen.)

Freeman, D. *A Rainbow of My Own*. New York: Penguin Books, 1978. (A child imagines enjoyable things to do with a rainbow.)

Kent, J. *The Grown-up Day*. New York: Parents Magazine, 1969. (Children pretend to be grown-ups.)

Krauss, R. *A Very Special House*. New York: Harper & Row, 1953. (Nonsense rhymes and pictures.)

LeSieg, T. *Wacky Wednesday*. New York: Beginner Books, 1974. (Find in the pictures the things that are silly.)

Lund, D. *Did You Ever?* New York: Parent's Magazine, 1965. (Silly things to try.)

McClosky, R. *Blueberries for Sal*. New York: Viking Press, 1976. (A little girl and a little bear get mixed up.)

Merriam, E. *That Noodlehead—Epaminondas*. New York: Scholastic Book Services, 1972. (A little boy gets his instructions mixed up.)

Meyer, M. *A Silly Story*. New York: Four Winds Press, 1972. (Boy's imagination makes him laugh. Charming pictures.)

Robinson, D. *Your Turn, Doctor*. New York: Dial Press, 1982. (A silly story about what a little girl says she would do if she were the doctor.)

Salus, N. *My Daddy's Mustache*. New York: Doubleday and Co., 1979. (A little boy's fun and delight with his daddy.)

Seuss, Dr. *There's a Wocket in My Pocket!* New York: Random House, 1974. (Nonsense words made up to rhyme.)

Slobodkina, E. *Caps for Sale*. New York: Scholastic Book Services, 1976. (A tale of a peddler, some monkeys, and some monkey business.)

Stone, J. *The Monster at the End of This Book.* Racine, Wisconsin: Western Publishing, 1976. (Grover, of Sesame Street, makes a silly mistake.)

Tester, S. *A Day of Surprises.* Chicago: Child's World, 1979. (Share a day of surprises with Saralinda.)

Wakefield, Joyce. *Ask a Silly Question.* Chicago: Childrens Press, 1979. (Silly answers and illustrations point out the difference between sound-alike words and phrases.)

Zolotow, C. *Not a Little Monkey.* New York: Lothrop, Lee, and Shephard, 1957. (Silly story to make you laugh.)

Teaching the Joy of the Body 2

"The body is an instrument for feeling. We choose much of what our bodies will feel. I want to choose joy."

I. Examples and Description

A. *Adult:* It wasn't that he was extraordinarily healthy; it was just that he enjoyed things about his physical body that most take for granted. He was a farmer, middle-aged, living in the flat, middle plain of America. He loved the hard, sweat-producing work in his field. "The hot sun limbers up my body," he would say, "makes me feel more loose and easy." He liked winter work as well. "My lungs like to feel that cold mornin' air a-fillin' 'em, and if I work hard enough, in ten minutes, I'm warm as summer."

On Wednesday evenings, after a long day's work, he played softball. He was the oldest member of the team. He said that part of the enjoyment was the competition and the company, but most of it was the physical joy. The catch, the throw, the hit—each, for him, was a momentary splurge of physical pleasures, a bump of joy.

The same physical joy showed in a different way when he took out his old fiddle. His tone was sometimes wrong—his position always was—but the rhythm in the twitch of shoulder and tap of toe plus his wide smile reflected uninhibited joy.

This man loved his senses and his senses loved the earth. He'd close his eyes so he could listen better to whippoorwills. He'd stop just to breathe the lilac breeze in early May. He'd let the soft, black soil sift through his fist just to feel its texture. And when his wife baked apple pie, he would hold the first bite in his mouth for half a minute "to be sure I taste it all."

He found amazement and wonder in the natural processes of his body—the rejuvenation of sleep, the fuel of food. Much of this world's progress and possessions had passed by this man, but his ability to feel the joy of his own body brightened his eye and enlivened his face so that the world looked back with envy.

B. *Child:* Here is a conversation I had with my three-year-old.

"Why do you have a body?"
"To skip with!"
"To skip with?"
"Yes."
"I see. What's the best part of your body?"

"The eyes."

"Why?"

"'Cause I see the flowers."

"Oh?"

"But the nose is too, 'cause I smell them."

"Do you hear them?"

"No, but if you close your eyes you do hear teensy little things."

"Like what?"

"Wind and trees."

"How do they sound?"

"Swish, swish, but quieter than that."

"Any other parts of the body you like?"

"The tongue to talk—you hold onto it and you can't talk— try it—say my name."

"Unghun—uwam."

"See!" (Laughter)

"Shawni, does your body make you happy?"

"My body *is* the happy!"

The spontaneous delight and built-in curiosity of little children make them receptive to the joy of the body. They are perfect pupils, but they still need teachers. The sensing equipment is built in—they receive the sensation—but they need to interpret it to feel its joy. A child's senses are more acute than ours, but the joy of the body lies in understanding what we sense, and that is where the teaching comes in.

What joy is in the body! The joy of work and of hard purposeful effort, the joy of singing, the joy of sport and activity, the joy of tenderness and physical touch, the joy of controlling physical things. Children have a tendency toward them all. Softly feel a baby's head, rough-house with a two-year-old, watch a three-year-old squeeze shapes from a square block of clay, and you'll see the opening melodies of the body's joy.

Inhibition and fear take away the body's joy. Children learn inhibitions and fear from us. How can we avoid it? First, we must help them to *try* physical things without intimidation, embarrassment, or fear. We must help them begin to sense the simple enjoyment of the functioning of their bodies. Then, beyond that, we must help them find and concentrate on the particular physical things that they do especially well, the things in which they are gifted, be they sports, music, crafts, dance, or whatever their own particular gifts suggest.

II. Methods

A. *Learning the names of body parts.*

*1. Play "Simon Says." The leader gives various commands: "Touch your tummy." "Lift your left foot." "Close your eyes." The rest of the players follow a command only if it is preceded by "Simon Says."

*2. Play "Hoky Poky." Players stand in a circle and act out this rhyme: "You put your left foot in, you put your left foot out, you put your left foot in and you shake it all about. You do the Hoky Poky and you turn yourself about. That's what it's all about—hey!" Rhyme is repeated with each part of body.

*3. Make a large puzzle of the body out of heavy cardboard pieces for children to put together. As they do, they name each part and tell what it can do.

B. *Teaching appreciation for the body.*

*1. Focus the children's attention on one sense: Have them close their eyes (or use a blindfold). Ask: "What can we hear? Listen closer—is there anything else we can hear?" (Do this outside and inside, in city and in country.)

Close your eyes and ears. What can we smell?

Close your eyes and ears. Taste something and identify it.

Close your eyes and ears. Feel something with your feet and identify it.

2. Pretend you don't have certain body parts, then try to do things. For example, pretend you have no fingers—just fists—and try to put on your shoes. With no eyes (blindfolded), try to put a piece in a puzzle. With no thumbs (tape them to fingers), try to pick up a penny. With only one hand (other one in pocket), try to catch a big ball. Without bending knees try to walk up stairs.

*3. "What is it?" game. Blindfold the children. Then let them hear and smell and touch and taste various things and try to identify them. Use things with interesting textures (sandpaper, cotton, polished stones); different sounds (bottled water, marbles in a box, a bell); distinct odors (perfume, popcorn, pickles); distinct tastes (sugar, salt, peanut butter, root beer).

*4. Identify sounds. Tape-record a variety of sounds; play them and have children identify what they are.

*5. Teach appreciation of the human body over other bodies. Pretend you are an elephant, bird, squirrel—what can you do? What can't you do? (Walk on two legs, pick up things with fingers, talk, walk while carrying something.) Now pretend you are a plant—what can't you do? (Almost everything.)

*6. Sensory stimulation. (a) Take a walk on a windy day. (b) Make popcorn in a popper with no lid (see page 12). Watch and listen while the popping corn spews out like a fountain (see it, smell it, hear it, feel it, taste it). Finger paint with chocolate pudding. This also uses all five senses.

*7. Teach how the body moves. What parts of the body can open and close? What parts of the body can bend? Shake? Twist? Can you make a "T" with your body? an "E"? a "C"? (Some letters require two children to make their shapes.)

8. Relate the senses to their uses. Make a chart with six columns. List the five senses across the top of the chart in columns two through six. Let the children pick items to list down the left column and put checks in the appropriate columns for the senses that perceive them. Examples: Winds—we hear it, feel it. A hot dog—we smell it, feel it, taste it, see it.

9. Talk about each activity afterward; recall it with glee. Say, "Wasn't it great to see which senses we use?" "Wasn't it fun to identify the sound?" Also, while the activity is actually taking place, try to find opportunities to say "Isn't this fun?" "Aren't our bodies great?" (Note: This is a key throughout the process of teaching children joy. During and after each experience with joy, help the child to identify the joy and be conscious that he is feeling it, so that he wants it and recognizes it the next time.)

C. *Use and development of bodily skills.*
*1. Dancing and marching. Use a variety of music, ranging from light, fairylike ballet pieces to heavy soldier marches. The stronger the rhythm the better. Encourage freedom of movement and lack of inhibition: "Try to kick the ceiling." "Look like a big tree swaying in the breeze." Most children can feel the mood of music; encourage them to let it out. Sometimes a partially darkened room helps children to feel more free. Use a particularly free, uninhibited child as an example.

*2. Learning to catch a ball. Few abilities give a child a greater sense of physical confidence and satisfaction. A large foam or sponge ball is easy to catch, a good first step. Also, teach children to shoot a basket; both boys and girls need the feeling of physical prowess and ability. Again, use a sponge ball with a low basket. Teach them that missing is just fine; take it all lightly.

3. Provide small, manipulative toys—things that fit together and that develop hand-to-eye coordination. Puzzles— very simple ones at first—are good. Lavish praise for each right move: "Isn't that great? You are so good at it!" (But be careful not to tell children they are good if they are not; if they can't do it yet, they can't feel the joy yet. Say, "I'll bet you can do it when you are four. Now let's find something else.")

*4. Provide balancing toys, such as swing sets and tumbling mats. Encourage—but don't push—exploration, swinging, hanging, climbing, jumping off.

*5. Teach simple songs and offer the children praise for singing. Tape-record their music and let them have the joy of listening to it again.

*6. Smelling game. Put different items in small containers, covering tightly with a piece of aluminum foil that is large enough to wrap the container completely. The children should not be able to see inside. Just before playing the smelling game, poke a hole in the top of each container with a pencil.

Suggested smelling items: tuna fish, onion (or onion salt), talcum powder, soap chips, pickle, cinnamon, dry mustard, cocoa.

For your convenience you may want to label each container with a piece of masking tape. Have children try to guess the contents.

*7. Tasting game. See if the children can taste well enough to identify foods that can be put directly into a child's hand to touch with his tongue, such as flavored gelatin, sugar, salt, or powdered drink mix. Or use foods that can be put directly in each child's mouth (with children blindfolded or closing eyes): peanut butter (on individual spoons or Popsicle sticks), small marshmallows, jam, honey, catsup, mustard.

*8. Hearing game. Record some common sounds and play them for the children. See if they can identify them:
—Doorbell ringing
—Telephone ringing
—Water agitating in the washing machine
—Corn popping
—Blowing of bubbles (straw in soap solution)
—Oven timer buzzing

—Car starting, windshield wipers working, horn honking
—Toilet flushing
—Dog barking, or other familiar animal sound
—Guitar, violin, or harmonica being played
—Vacuum cleaner running
—Baby crying
—The Joy School group at play (if you can tape it without their noticing it)

*9. Five senses game. Prepare ahead of time by putting several different items in small paper bags. Close each bag and put all the small bags into a large box. Have children try to identify each item by sound, touch, smell, sight, and taste as it comes out of the box.

With each item, first shake it to see if the children's ears can tell them what it is. Then try the other senses in the order suggested after each item:

—Sponge: hear, feel, guess what color, see
—Bar of soap: hear, smell, see (cut a one-inch hole in the side of the bag to smell through)
—Hairbrush or toothbrush: hear, feel, see
—Empty, unwashed tuna can: hear, smell, see (cut a one-inch hole in the side of the bag to smell through)
—Sugar in a covered dish: hear, see, taste (is it salt or sugar?)
—Bottle of red punch: hear, see, smell, taste (what flavor?)
—Cotton: hear, feel, see
—Bell: hear, see
—Two or three marbles in a small box: hear, see

*10. What can your body do? Sit on the floor with the children. Talk about what parts of your body can open and close (eyes, mouth, hands, arms, legs, and so on). Do each thing with the children, one part at a time. Then slowly "close" your whole body (naming one part at a time) into a tight ball. Now let the whole body "open" (extend) slowly, one part at a time. Try closing and opening fast, like an explosion. Help the children to feel and enjoy the things their bodies can do.

Stand up and talk about the ways your body can move around the room. Lead the children in movements such as walking, running (in place), hopping, jumping, skipping, galloping, and walking backward or sideways. Let the children suggest some.

*11. Outside obstacle course. If your yard conditions per-

mit, set up outside some of the following things to form an obstacle course:

—A six- to eight-foot-long 2x4 beam, set up on two bricks
(one on each end) for the children to walk along

—Old tires, laid down in a row, to walk on or in

—A rope stretched between two trees, eight or ten inches
from the ground to jump over

—A large inflated inner tube to climb over

—Large cardboard cartons with one end open and a hole
cut in the other end or the top for the children to crawl into
and climb out of

—A board (ten or twelve inches wide and six to eight feet
long) with one end on the ground and the other end raised up
on something: to use as a ramp to walk up and jump from

—Bricks or wooden blocks as stepping stones

—If you have a slide, work it into the sequence

—Anything else that is suitable

Be creative. Look around your yard or garage for additional ideas. Be sure the materials are free of slivers, nails, or
other hazards and are on a safe surface so the children will not
get hurt if they fall. Caution the children against pushing.
Everyone should go in the same direction.

*12. "Body" rhythm band. Seat the children in a circle
and ask them to tell you some of the sounds they can make
with their bodies (other than using voices). If they are not re-
sponding, ask questions. "What sounds can your hands make?
your feet? your tongue?" You name those that they don't
think of: clapping, snapping fingers, swishing hands together,
slapping thighs, thumping chest, tapping toes, stamping,
clicking tongue, making a popping sound with lips. As each
sound is named, have all the children try it. Then say, "Let's
have a rhythm band. I will play some marching music and we
can march around and play our 'body instruments.'" Tell the
children to choose which "instrument" they will use and to
change "instruments" whenever they like.

Play some music with a suitable rhythm for marching, and
be sure to join in the parade.

Always give total encouragement and praise. A negative
word can ruin fragile physical confidence and delay or thwart
the very physical joy you are trying to create and teach. If the
result is good, praise the result: "You did skip!" "You sang that

right on tune!" If the result is not good, praise the attempt, the effort: "What a good try! Before long you'll do it!"

D. *Care of the body.*

1. Show children two cars: one clean and well cared for, with plenty of good gas and oil, and the other one broken down. Ask them which car they would rather have. Ask them how each owner took care of his car. Compare the cars to our bodies: gas and oil—good food; clean outside—regular baths; clean inside—brushed teeth; good tires—lots of exercise; bright headlights—enough sleep.

2. Show children pictures of two people: one an "in-shape" athlete, one a sagging, out-of-shape person. List the things one does that the other doesn't do: exercises, eats good food, keeps himself clean, gets enough sleep.

3. Identify "healthful" and "sometimes" foods. You will need a flannelboard, a piece of yarn to divide the flannelboard into two sections, and several food pictures cut from magazines (colored ones are best). Prepare each picture for the flannelboard by gluing a piece of flannel on the back. Put the pictures in a box.

Ask the children to tell you some foods that help them to be well and strong. Then ask them to name some foods that taste good but that we should eat only after meals and not too often (candy, cake, pop, cookies, and other sweets). Then say, "In this box I have some pictures of foods that are very good for you and also some foods that we will call 'sometimes foods,' those that we should not eat too much of. This side of the flannelboard will be for healthful foods and this side for 'sometimes foods.'"

III. Family Focal Point: The Family Activity Board

There is something special about a family that does physical things together. There is something special about any relationship that is partially born out of shared physical activity. We learn when we play ball with someone, swim with someone; the activity brings the minds together, relaxes the atmosphere, and opens up the communication. This is doubly true in families. Families that play together stay together.

Our family has a list on a big, paper-covered bulletin board that we call "The Family Activity Board." Any family member, upon thinking of a physical or sports activity that he would like to do with the family, jots it down on the list with a big circle by it. Anticipation builds until a free night comes along when we can all do the activity. When it does, the circle is colored in.

We have defined what kinds of things can go on the board: things we can do together as a family that let our bodies stretch and exercise and feel good. Even the little ones understand. The list has become a rather interesting mixture of the conventional and the unconventional. It has included bowling, swimming, canoeing, sand-surfing at the dunes, walking to school instead of driving, bike riding all the way to Burke Lake, hiking in the Appalachians in the fall, using the stopwatch and setting "records" for running around the block, and having Mom show us her yoga.

On one section of the activity board, we've put a "family records list"—the fastest time for running around the block, for skipping rope around the block, and so on. This charts the children's improvement and teaches the joy of progressing and excelling physically.

IV. Story: "Ben, the Rich Boy"

Once there was a boy named Ben. He was a strong and healthy lad. But he thought he was very, very poor because he had no money. When he saw people with money and fine things, it made him want to be rich.

Ben knew that there were four very rich men in the land. One day he decided that he would visit each of them and ask them how to be rich.

The first man lived on a hill in the northern part of the land. Ben asked him how to become rich. The man said, "Look out my window and tell me what you see." Ben looked out and saw beautiful red and orange leaves, because it was autumn. He saw blue sky, and purple, snow-capped mountains in the distance. He saw a hummingbird pausing at hollyhocks to collect honey. He told the man what he saw. "You are rich," said the man, "because of everything that your eyes can see." Ben left the first man's house. He wanted to be rich, and if that man wouldn't tell him how, he would find someone else who would.

The second rich man lived in a valley in the eastern part of the land. He was an old man with a long beard. Ben asked him how to become rich. The old man looked at Ben and said, "How did you get to my house?" "I walked from the north," said Ben. "Then you are rich," said the man. "You are rich because you have strong legs—you can walk and dance and skip and jump and run. I am old and lame. I would give every penny I have if I could walk like you." And Ben wondered why the man wouldn't tell him what he wanted to know.

Then Ben went to the third man's house, which was in a city in the southern part of the land. The man was out on his patio. Ben introduced himself and said, "Would you tell me how to become wealthy?" The man looked at Ben for a long time, then said, "Do you hear the crickets in my bush?" Ben said, "Yes." "Do you smell the food that is cooking?" "Yes." "Then you are rich. My senses are dim. I know of the sounds and smells only because I remember them. I cannot taste or feel or smell or hear as clearly as you. If I could, I would gladly give every penny I have." Again Ben wondered why the man wouldn't tell him what he wanted to know.

The last man lived in a castle in the western part of the land. Ben went to him and said, "You are my last hope. Will you tell me how to be rich?" "But you must be rich," said the man. "Look at the fine shirt you wear." "This?" said Ben. "I had to make this shirt with my own hands and sew it with the thread made from the wool of my sheep." "Then you are rich. Your hands can make shirts and paint pictures and play musical instruments. My hands are old and shake so much that I can do none of these things. If I could, I would give every penny I have."

Ben left the man and started to go home. None of the men had told him how to be rich. All they had told him was that he was rich already because of his body and the things it could do. As Ben walked, the sun shone warmly on his back, and he heard the birds and animals around him and saw the flowers along his way. Perhaps he was rich. Maybe his body and the things he could be were worth more than money.

What do you think?

V. Reading List (Including Out-of-print Titles)

Aliki, *My Five Senses*. New York: Harper and Row, 1972. (Introduce children to the five senses and how they help us to be aware of everything around us.)

Baylor, B. *Sometimes I Dance Mountains*. New York: Charles Scribner's Sons, 1973. (A little girl enjoys using her body in creative movement.)

Brown, M., and S. Krensky. *Dinosaurs Beware! A Safety Guide.* New York: Little, Brown and Co., 1982.

Johnston, D. G. *Stop, Look, Listen.* Cincinnati, Ohio: Standard Publishing, 1977. (Father and child take time to enjoy the things that their senses help them to be aware of.)

Kraus, R. *The Growing Story.* New York: Harper and Row, 1947. (Delightful story about how a little boy finds out he is growing bigger.)

Marshall, J. *Yummers!* New York: Houghton Mifflin, 1973.

McGuire, L. *You, Your Body, How It Works.* New York: Platt and Munk, 1974. (Colorful pictures and descriptive text about body parts, how they work, and how to keep healthy.)

Merriam, E. *Andy All Year Round.* New York: Funk and Wagnalls, 1969. (Andy's wonderful body helps him enjoy the seasons.)

Moncure, J. *About Me.* Chicago: Child's World, 1976. (The wonder of hands, feet, eyes, ears, and how they bring us joy.)

————. *Magic Monsters Learn About Health.* Chicago: Childrens Press, 1980. (Magic Monsters learn how important good nutrition, sleep, and exercise are.)

Peterson, G. *Fun and Discovering with Your Five Senses.* Kansas City, Missouri: Hallmark Cards, 1977. (How each of the senses helps us learn about and enjoy life.)

Showers, P. *Find Out by Touching.* New York: Harper and Row, 1961. (How our sense of touch can help us find out about things. A "Let's read and find out" science book.)

————. *Follow Your Nose.* New York: Harper and Row, 1975. (About the sense of smell.)

————. *The Listening Walk.* New York: Harper and Row, 1961. (Sounds you might hear as you go for a walk.)

————. *Look at Your Eyes.* New York: Harper and Row, 1976. (About the sense of sight.)

Tudor, Tasha. *Five Senses.* (Originally titled *First Delights.*) New York: Platt and Munk, 1978. (A little girl enjoys the senses each season of the year.)

Walt Disney's Healthy, Happy Pooh Book. New York: Golden Press, 1977. (Pooh and friends teach how to be healthy and happy.)

Watson, J. *My Body, How It Works.* New York: Golden Press, 1972. (About body parts, inside and out—what they are for and how they work.)

Ziegler, Sandra. *At the Dentist—What Did Christopher See?*
Chicago: Child's World, 1976. (Go along with Christopher
as he learns about his teeth.)

Records:

Brady, Janeen. *Watch Me Sing.* Salt Lake City: Brite Enter-
prises.

Hap Palmer Record Library, Educational Activities, Inc., Box
392, Freeport, N.Y.: *Creative Movement and Rhythm Expression* (AR 533); *Getting to Know Myself* (AR 543); *Learning
Basic Skills through Music* (AR 514); *Movin'* (AR 546).

Teaching
the
Joy of 3
the Earth

"If spring came but once in a century instead of once a year, or burst forth with the sound of an earthquake and not in silence, what wonder and expectation there would be in all hearts to behold the miraculous change." (Henry Wadsworth Longfellow.)

I. Examples and Description

A. *Adult:* Flat green, tilted mountainside darker greens, rocky mountaintop grays—I drink these in as the plane descends to land in Jackson Hole. Half an hour later I'm fishing in a clear brook. To my back stretches the soft, morning-lighted forest. Long, late-July grass carpets the ground below the large spruce; a smaller fir grows to my left. The downstream surface of the brook faintly flickers, reflecting light green trees at the back, dark green mountains in the middle, and blue sky in front of me.

Across the stream lies the Snake River Valley, and behind it, the Teton range. White, midsummer glaciers mark the crags and shaded spots in the jutting rock. A hawk floats, wing-tip feathers spread, across my field of vision. To my right, upstream, rise the Grand Tetons themselves, drawing the eye with an excitement that speeds the heart. They push through the only clouds in the sky. (A lonely cloud often sits there as if caught and held by the peaks.)

When I shut my eyes to make more of my brain available to my ears, I hear two ripples in the stream: one just upstream in my right ear and the other downstream in my left—stereophonic sound!

And the birds. I count five different kinds of chirps—only one that I know, the meadow lark's rhythmic, "Ain't I a pretty-little-bird?"

Once in a while a plane can be heard droning in the distance, and occasionally a cricket's rasp, behind and tucked between the other sounds.

One can't describe the smell. It combines so much—the grass, the trees, the sage—floating on air as clear and cool as the water in the stream. They seem so similar, the air and water: both clear, both cool, both fresh, both flowing.

I guess one reason I love Jackson so much is the seasons—the change, the transition, and the fact that, since I come only five or six times a year, the changes are distinct rather than gradual. One time (early summer) it will be like the day at the brook. Next time (early autumn) brings Indian summer, when cottonwoods start to turn color, Snake River starts to turn clear, air starts to turn crisp, and sagebrush mountainsides look like scuffed buckskin against the sky's deeper blue. Next time it's late fall: the mantle of golden quaking aspen filters and softens the sun's more slanted rays. Flamelike cottonwoods pull forth the valley's deep purples and the cloud's fleecy white. The air is even crisper, almost tart. Then I come again in midwinter to ski; to sit alone in a soft snowstorm on a split-rail fence; to hear the silence of the white world; to see the fleecy, buffeting flakes building into quiet, white mounds around the darker, colder, half-ice streams; to feel the whole vibrant world settle and sleep.

There is such beauty in the earth. Joy comes through sensing it—with all five senses. I remember a poet I knew who wrote mostly of the earth, who saw so much in the world that I didn't see. He had a sign on his wall that said: "Five Sense Sagacity." I asked him about it. He said that *serendipity*, which means happy accidents, pleasant surprises, comes about through *sagacity*, which means acute awareness, appreciation, sensitivity, which in turn comes about through applied, thorough use of all five senses. Think about that for a moment; it is quite a message: Happiness comes through awareness.

Joy and opportunity lie in the appreciation of the earth's beauties. So often we miss these joys—not because the earth lacks beauty (for indeed, every part of it is beautiful, but because of our apathy, our failure to see and to notice, our tendency to take it for granted.

B. *Child:* Our son Josh was fifteen months old and it was April. The summer before, he had been too small to be outside much, so, on this first warm day of the year, he was seeing the backyard for the first time. I watched him in silence from the window. He started with the grass, first feeling it, then sitting down in it, moving his legs back and forth, so delighted that he laughed aloud. Then he lay down, mouth open with an expression of anticipation, as he felt the grass with the back of his head and neck. From that position he noticed the sky and the clouds. He lifted both arms, pointed both forefingers, formed a round O with his little mouth, and said, with a tone of reverence and amazement, "Oooh!" There was a spring breeze moving those fluffy clouds across the deep blue sky. He watched almost motionlessly for two or three minutes until the wind started to gust a little and he became more interested in the cool, feathery breeze on his skin. He stood up, turned his face into the breeze, squinted, gritted his teeth, and uttered his second descriptive sound, "Eeeh."

Turning in a new direction, he noticed a small patch of tiny white and yellow flowers in the grass. Toddling over, he reached down to pick one. The stem was fairly stiff, and as it broke, he fell back on his bottom into a sitting position. From there he held the flower close to his face and pulled off one tiny petal with his thumb and forefinger—a use of his hands he had recently discovered. When he had finished, he threw his little arms up, let the rest of the flower go at the top, and brought his hands slapping down on his knees with a contented sigh.

Then a bird chirped in the nearby tree. Josh cocked his head, a little startled, not sure where the sound had come from. The bird chirped again. This time Josh saw where it was. He stood up and toddled toward the tree. The bird swooped down, floated twenty yards or so, and landed on the lawn. Josh followed the flight with a look of delight and utter amazement. As he watched, motionless, the bird began his staccato pecking at the grass and an instant later pulled up a squirming, wiggling worm. Josh shook his head, as if in disbelief, and started shuffling toward the bird. The bird fluttered back up into the tree, chirping all the way.

Josh repeated his earlier cloud gesture, pointing up at the bird with both hands and saying, "Oooh!"

II. Methods

A. *Teach the earth's terminology.*

1. Look together at large picture books of animals, trees, and flowers. Point to a picture and have the children say the name, or you say the name and have them point.

2. Point at things in nature wherever you go—point and say the names.

3. Involve the children in picnics, nature walks, exposure to the out-of-doors. At zoos or botanical gardens, or at home in the backyard, notice nature. Talk about it; ask the children to tell about it.

B. *Teach deep appreciation for the earth.*

1. Focus attention on one small sight or one small sound. Have the children look through paper tubes (from paper towels or toilet tissue) so they have one small field of vision. Ask, "What do you see? Can you describe it? Isn't it beautiful?" Now have the children close their eyes. Pick out small, individual sounds and ask, "Can you hear that?"

*2. Use the "senses chart" again from the previous chapter; however, this time focus attention on things from nature in the left vertical column rather than the senses in the top horizontal column.

3. Take nature walks. You don't have to be in the woods or mountains; a vacant field or a park will do. Point out things, but without too much explanation let the children explore. If you find an ant hill, stop to watch. Ask what the ants are doing. Ask lots of questions to help the children figure things out. Take nature walks to the same place in all four seasons, and ask: "How have things changed?"

*4. Put an ant colony in a glass case. The ants will make tunnels and the children can watch them work.

5. Teach children to distinguish nature from nonnature. On nature walks, ask them to find things that are not nature's—cans, paper, litter—and pick them up. Point out that man's things are not as beautiful as those in nature; show that each little thing in nature is unique, while man's things are often mass-produced.

*6. Make a see-through "growing bottle" by putting wet, crumpled paper towels into a bottle with seeds between the glass and the moist paper. Set it where it gets sunlight. Watch as roots grow down and leaves and shoots grow up.

7. Watch ants and bugs with the children and be interested in them instead of smashing them.

8. Paste up a collage from each season. Look through magazines together for pictures: "Here's something for winter—here are pictures of autumn leaves for fall."

*9. Make four-season collections—nature things picked up from each season. Gather autumn seeds and grain from fall, flowers from spring, bare branches from winter.

10. Watch and feed birds.

11. Have pets. Learn about them and how to take care of them. Some areas have pet libraries from which children can check out a pet for a week.

12. Listen to classical music, and tell what things from nature your mind sees as you listen.

13. Take pictures of beautiful things the children point out—or let them snap their own pictures. Enjoy the experiences again when you see the prints or slides.

14. Expose children to the arts. Take them to galleries, concerts, and museums.

*15. Fill a box (such as a produce box with low sides) with sand or dirt. Make a pond in it with blue paper, and use small twigs with leaves or evergreens to make a little forest. Talk with the children about how different parts of the earth are used for different animals' homes. With the children's help, place small toy animals or pictures of animals mounted on toothpicks in their appropriate homes in the box.

C. *Teach the joys of the use of nature.*

*1. Get a small, simple loom to make cloth from wool.

*2. Milk a cow; drink the milk and make butter. Gather eggs and cook them.

*3. Gather wheat, take the chaff off yourself, grind the wheat, make dough, bake bread.

*4. Play a question-and-answer game about the uses of nature: "What can you do or make with a tree? with sand? with a cow?"

*5. Have a nature meal, with honey, eggs, milk, and home-baked bread.

6. Walk through the supermarket and see if the children can tell where different foods come from and how nature provides them. Walk by clothing displays and have them tell you the same things about the cloth.

*7. While the question of "where things come from" is still on the children's minds, place some of the following objects in a box. Set or hold it high enough that the children cannot see inside. Give each child a turn to reach in and take out one object and then try to tell where it comes from. Give what explanations are necessary.

carrot	can of tuna	cereal	wood
banana	honey	hot dog	glass
apple	milk	cotton	paper
bread	raisins	woolen mitten	

*8. Play a "riddle game" with children. Say, "I'm thinking of something that is part of our wonderful world. I'll tell you some things about it and then you see if you can guess what it is that I'm thinking about. If you think you know, raise your hand, but don't say anything until I say, 'What is it?'"

—"I'm thinking of something that is green. It grows. Sometimes it is small. Sometimes it grows very tall. It has leaves. Sometimes fruit grows on it. What is it?" (A tree.)

—"I'm thinking of something that is up in the sky. It is white. We see it mostly at night. It is round. It shines and gives us light. What is it?" (The moon.)

—"I'm thinking of something that is about this big (show with hands). It could be black or white or gray or yellow. It is soft and furry. It has a tail. It has whiskers. It can creep very quietly. It purrs and says 'Meow.' What is it?" (A cat or kitten.)

—"I'm thinking of something that smells fresh. People need it. Animals need it. Flowers and trees need it. Fish need it. It is wet. It falls from the sky. What is it?" (Rain.)

—"I'm thinking of something that you cannot see, but you can feel it. Sometimes it is cool. Sometimes it is warm. It can move the trees. It can fly a kite. Sometimes it says 'oo-oo-ooo.' What is it?" (Wind.)

—"I'm thinking of some things that come in many shapes, sizes, and colors. They grow in the woods, in gardens, in houses, in the fields. They smell good. Bees like them. They make our world beautiful. What are they?" (Flowers.)

—"I'm thinking of something that is the most beautiful and important part of our wonderful world. It is about this high (show). It grows. Every one is different. It has eyes. It has two arms and two legs that can walk or run or skip or jump. It can sing. It can talk. What is it?" (A child.)

III. Family Focal Point: The Family Favorite Things Wall

About the time our Saren turned three, her artistic talents becoming more manifest each day, she took to drawing on the walls. We tried various means to dissuade her from this practice, but our efforts were tempered by the creativity and beauty of her "artwork" and by the fact that she seemed to have far more interest in the walls than in paper, blackboard, or anything else we could provide.

Finally, in desperation, we designated one wall in the den, where nobody but our family goes, for drawing on. It consequently became known as the drawing room. Saren confined her efforts to that wall and, before long, its lower half was covered with faces and shapes of all description.

Not long after this, we held a special family council on "favorite things." We were thinking of the small, simple things in life that give us pleasure: snowflakes, kites, crackling fires, the opening day of fishing season, single roses, the sound of crisp apples being dumped into a box, the sound of the woodpecker behind our house. The list kept growing, but we had nowhere to put it except on that wall.

Since that night we've called it the "favorite things wall." Whenever someone notices something he enjoys, something that gives him a spark of pure joy, he writes it on the wall, thus sharing it and, through sharing, remembering it. (Children who are too young to write can draw their favorite things.) The wall became so valuable to us over the years that when we rented the house to someone else, we actually included in the rental agreement a clause prohibiting any redecorating or painting over those favorite things.

IV. Story: "Earth Ernie"

Ernie was playing alone in his backyard with a little dump truck and a steam shovel. All at once he heard a whirling noise, and when he looked up, he saw a purple, round spinning thing that looked like a big plate. Ernie knew that it was a spaceship. (He had seen pictures.)

A hatch in the bottom opened, and out climbed a small, purple man. Ernie knew right away that he was friendly because he was smiling. "Hi," said Ernie, because he was friendly too. When the purple man said, "Hello, Ernie," it made Ernie think of two questions. One was, "How did you know my name?" and the other was, "How do you know how to speak English?" The little purple man said it was because he had been listening from his planet through his "ear telescope," which made faraway sounds easy to hear. "I came to see you," said the little purple man, "because you are one of the nicest people I've listened to. I'd like you to come for a ride with me to my planet. Our king is too old to travel, and he would like to meet an earth person."

Now Ernie would *never* get in a car with a stranger. He knew better than that. But this was a cute little purple man in a *spaceship*.

"Well," said Ernie, "I sure would like to ride in your flying saucer and see your world, but my mother would worry about me."

"No, she won't," said the little purple man. "My spaceship goes faster than time, so I can have you right back here in your backyard before she even knows you've gone."

When Ernie heard that, he climbed in behind the little purple man.

The ride was fun. Ernie got to drive the spaceship part of the way. It had a steering wheel like a car. The ship went very fast, and once the little purple man, who told Ernie his name was Thoyd, had to take the steering wheel because Ernie nearly hit a star.

Before long the ship slowed down, and Ernie could see a round, flat, shiny purple world. "There's my planet," said Thoyd. "Isn't it pretty?" "Yes," said Ernie, "so shiny and flat." "It's made out of purple plastic," said Thoyd. "Plastic?" said Ernie. "Yes, we made it," said Thoyd. "We used to have a world like yours, but the air and water got so dirty and there was so much garbage everywhere that we had to make ourselves this new one."

"But where are your trees and your animals, Thoyd?"

"Oh, we don't have those things anymore. They don't grow on plastic. We have synthetic food. It comes in six flavors and looks a little like toothpaste."

"But do you have any mountains to climb or lakes to float in?"

"No," said Thoyd, "we lost those too, but this purple plastic world is great for roller skating." Thoyd went to get the king, and Ernie looked around. The air smelled like plastic. There were no flowers or grass, no fields or hills or rocks, no sounds of birds or babbling brooks or wind in the trees; there were no farm animals or cold milk or fresh eggs; no ears of corn to pick or potatoes to dig; not even any sand or soil. The blue sky didn't look as pretty as it should next to the shiny purple horizon.

Pretty soon Thoyd came back with a very old-looking little purple man who had a purple plastic crown and a long beard. Thoyd said, "This is King Pele. He is the only purple man old enough to remember our old world—and he has a message for you." The old king came up close to Ernie, held Ernie's hand, and leaned his mouth close to Ernie's ear. "Earth Ernie," said the old king in a faint, gruff whisper, "tell your people to know and love their earth, or they will lose it like we lost ours." The old king patted Ernie's shoulder and smiled at him; then he slowly walked away.

"Do you want to stay and have a tour of our world?" asked Thoyd. "No, thanks," said Ernie. He just wanted to get back to his beautiful earth to make sure it was still there. "I understand," said Thoyd, and they got back on the flying saucer.

They seemed to go slower on the way back, and Ernie wanted to get back so badly. Finally they landed in his backyard, and, just as Thoyd had said, Ernie's mother was still inside and everything was just as they had left it.

As soon as Thoyd was gone, Ernie ran to get his mother and his little sister, Sue. "Come," he said, taking each of their hands. "Where are we going, Ernie?" "To the park," said Ernie. For the next hour, Ernie showed his mother the trees and grass, the flowers and bushes. They smelled roses, patted dogs, listened to every sound that nature made, and even picked up every scrap of litter they could find.

"We need to love our world, Mommy. Otherwise we'll lose it." Mother didn't know what had gotten into Ernie, but she agreed with him anyway.

V. Reading List (Including Out-of-print Titles)

Bancroft, H. *Down Come the Leaves.* New York: Harper and Row, 1961. (What happens in the fall? A "Let's read and find out" book.)

De Regniers, B. *Who Likes the Sun?* New York: Harcourt Brace Jovanovich, 1961. (The pleasures and importance of the sun.)

De Rico, U. *The Rainbow Goblins.* New York: Warner Books, 1983.

Ets, M. H. *Gilberto and the Wind.* New York: Viking Press, 1963. (A little boy's relationship with the wind.)

Freschet, B. *The Web in the Grass.* New York: Charles Scribner's Sons, 1972. (A delightful and informative story about spiders.)

Hawkinson, J. *Robins and Rabbits.* Chicago: Albert Whitman, 1960. (Brief text and lovely pictures of woodland creatures.)

Hoberman, M. *A House Is a House for Me.* New York: Penguin Press, 1982.

Keats, E. J. *The Snowy Day*. New York: Viking Press, 1962. (A child's delight in discovering snow.)

Krauss, R. *The Happy Day*. New York: Harper and Row, 1980. (The joys of the coming of spring.)

Langstaff, J. *Over in the Meadow*. New York: Harcourt Brace Jovanovich, 1967. (A counting book with good nature pictures.)

Lewis, R. *The Park*. New York: Simon and Schuster, 1968. (Beautiful photographs of nature scenes.)

Martin, D. *The Apple Book*. Racine, Wisconsin: Western Publishing, 1964. (Discusses the wonderful fruits of nature.)

McGovern, A. *Who Has a Secret?* Boston; New York: Houghton Mifflin, 1964. (About the "secrets" of nature.)

Merriam, E. *Andy All Year Round*. New York: Funk and Wagnalls, 1967. (Being aware of and enjoying the seasons.)

Miller, E. *Mouskin's ABC's*. New Jersey: Prentice Hall, 1972. (Lovely nature pictures. Text in rhyme.)

Moncure, J. *Spring Is Here!* Chicago: Child's World, 1975. (Beautifully illustrated. Helps children be aware of seasonal changes.)

———. *Thank You, Animal Friends*. Chicago: Child's World, 1975. (Expresses gratitude for the useful products animals give us.)

———. *What Causes It?* Chicago: Child's World, 1977. (Answers children's questions about the weather.)

———. *What Will It Be?* Chicago: Child's World, 1976. (How animals and plants reproduce.)

Myers, B. *Charlie's Birthday Present*. New York: Scroll Press, 1981. (Boy discovers how wonderful a tree is.)

O'Neill, Mary. *Hailstorms and Halibut Bones*. New York: Doubleday, 1961. (Lovely poetry about the sight, sound, smell, feel, and taste of colors in nature.)

Parnall, P. *The Mountain*. New York: Doubleday, 1971. (Thought-provoking story about the pollution of the earth.)

Parr, L. *When Sea and Sky Are Blue*. New York: Scroll Press, 1971. (A child experiences the joy of nature.)

Pienkowski, J. *Weather*. New York: Simon and Schuster, 1983.

Poulet, V. *Blue Bug's Beach Party*. Chicago: Childrens Press, 1975. (Leads to discussion about littering.)

Provenson, A. and M. *A Book of Seasons*. New York: Random House, 1978. (The joy of the ever-changing seasons.)

Ranger Rick's Nature Magazine. National Wildlife Federation (12 issues per year), 1412 16th St. N.W., Washington, D.C., 20036.

Spiers, P. *Rain.* New York: Doubleday, 1982.

Shulevitz, U. *Rain Rain Rivers.* New York: Farrar, Straus and Giroux, 1969. (Lovely pictures and comments about the joys of rain.)

Udry, J. M. *A Tree Is Nice.* New York: Harper and Row, 1956. (Discusses the many securities, needs, and pleasures that a tree provides for us.)

Watson, J. W. *The Wonders of Nature.* New York: Golden Press, 1958. (Simple text, lovely pictures about nature.)

MENTAL JOYS

"The entire object of true education is to make people not merely to do the right things, but enjoy them; not merely industrious, but to love industry; not merely learned, but to love knowledge; not merely pure, but to love purity; not merely just, but to hunger and thirst after justice." (John Ruskin.)

Too often we perceive the mind only as an instrument of survival, wisdom, or power. It is too easy to forget that the mind is an instrument of joy.

We not only perceive the joy of the earth and body with the mind, we employ the powers of the mind to give us the joys of learning, of imagining, of creating, of deciding, and of achieving goals.

Children possess the capacities for seemingly endless forms of mental joy. But these joys must be experienced to be learned. A child's mind has been likened to a computer with massive capacity, most of which has yet to be programmed. The teaching methods in this section are designed to increase the joy in a child's mental circuitry, to help his natural curiosity grow into imagination and creativity, to show him the satisfaction of orderliness and of setting and achieving goals, and to give him the mental skills and discipline to obey laws and make sound decisions.

Preserving the Joy of Interest and Curiosity 4

Ah, to see the world through the eyes of a child, where there is wonder in all things and where boredom or routine do not exist.

I. Examples and Description

A. *Child:* I remember sitting once, off to the side in a busy shopping mall, looking at passing people—watching to see who was watching. The adults were preoccupied with their jobs, their problems, themselves. Their eyes never met mine. Their eyes saw only what was necessary to navigate through the crowded corridor.

But the children saw everything. Each child looked straight at me for at least a moment, and for a moment at everything. Their eyes and ears were receptors, taking in all the data, seeing, hearing, questioning.

It is no wonder that we learn as much in our first five years as in the rest of our lives. We see more, feel more. We are born with a natural and joyful curiosity and interest. What happens to it? Where did those adults drop it? When would those children lose theirs?

One study showed that babies spend one-fifth of their waking hours in motionless, focused gazing, simply figuring things out with their eyes. Their minds are so malleable, so impressionable! Parents can perhaps change their children's minds more, for better or for worse, than they can change either their bodies or their spirits.

B. *Adult:* I had been a student in Boston for two years. I loved the city and thought I knew it pretty well. Then a visitor came to spend a weekend with us on his way through the city. "What do you want to do?" I asked. "See Boston!" he said. I took him to my favorite places: the Wharf, Hay Market Square, the Freedom Trail. His eyes were wide the whole day. His comments were of fascination, even awe. "That really happened here?" His questions were questions of genuine interest, questions of history, of geography, of personality, of joyful curiosity. I couldn't answer most of them because I had never asked them. In those two days I think I saw more reflected in his eyes than I had seen in two years through my own eyes.

I thought I loved Boston, but my friend enjoyed the tour, enjoyed the day, the people, the smells, the feelings, more than I had the first time I had seen them or at any time since. The joy that I saw in his face was the involved, absorbed, wrapped-up, forget-himself-and-his-own-problems joy of curiosity and of interest. He had, preserved within him, a joy that nearly all small children possess and nearly all adults lose.

II. Methods

A. *Learn from children's example; participate with and encourage them.* My wife and I observed our three-year-old through the back window playing alone among the flowers on a warm, early-spring day. Her delight and intense interest showed so clearly that we felt it, and I murmured, "How can we keep that in her forever?" My wife replied, "By watching her watching, and watching what she watches."

Since then, we have come to know that that's the secret. Children are the teachers, the experts; we are the learners, the students. The teachers can be encouraged by the interest of the learners, and thus their interest-expertise can gain the element of pride that causes it to remain. Chances for application come daily: instead of pulling them away from their activity (jumping in leaves) and into yours (cleaning house), how about occasionally leaving *yours* to join them in *theirs?* (Don't worry, the leaves will brush out of your hair.)

B. *Answer and ask.* While you are in those leaves, your teacher (your child) may ask, "Did a caterpillar make this hole in this leaf?" You might consider these responses: thanking him for teaching you to have an interest in that hole; answering him by saying, "Yes, a caterpillar probably did"; and opening a chance for more teaching by asking, "And where do you suppose that caterpillar is right now?"

How precious a question is! An alert mind that asks is the first step to answers, discoveries, solutions. Never ignore or criticize a question; this is like stepping on a flower bud just set to bloom. The moment a question is asked is like the moment a flower blooms on an early spring morning. The air is clean and crisp, the images precise and distinct. The child's mind is ready to absorb; the moment won't last. So many people— running, hurrying, preoccupied—walk past the flower, drive right through the spring morning without seeing or smelling it, and the moment passes, forever lost. The child asks and we defer, brush off, hurry the answer, or, even worse, say, "Don't bother me now, I'm busy." Oh, the need to go the other direction—to praise the question, to flatter him for asking it, to help a child glory in his wonderings!

Actually, to go back to the analogy, two mistakes are commonly made as the flower blooms on the new spring morning. One is to miss it, walk past it, never see it; the other is to *pick* it instead of appreciating it, enjoying it, helping if we can to make it grow.

With a questioning child, one of two similar mistakes usually occurs: (1) ignoring, brushing off, not noticing the beauty and potential of that moment, and (2) answering instead of reasoning together, helping, or asking questions of the child that will help him answer his own. When we take the time to discuss a question, we help the child to understand the wonderful concepts of reasoning, conceptualizing, researching— the ideas that allow him to glory in his wonderings and rejoice in discovered answers.

C. *Respond to your child's initiative.* A well-documented university study reveals something few would expect: that parents of the smartest children don't try to teach them all the time, but try to teach only when the child wants to learn. The study took students from apparently similar backgrounds, all from good families, upper-middle-class homes, nonworking mothers, with no apparent hereditary differences and no apparent emotional differences. One subgroup had high I.Q.s and high grades, while the other had lower grades and lower I.Q.s. The object of the study was to determine where the difference first occurred, where the smart got smart and vice versa.

The researchers went back a year at a time, looking for differences. They didn't find any until they got to the preschool years at home. The difference was the mothers. Mothers of the high I.Q. and good-grade children (the "A" mothers) were *consultants.* They loved their children, but they let them develop in their own way. They gave freedom, an interesting environment, and time, but not all their time. They had a wide variety of other interests besides their children. They painted, they took violin lessons, or they played tennis, but they recognized teaching moments and taught what their children were interested in *when* they were interested in it. They gave the initiative to their children.

The "C" mothers overtaught, overprotected, and over supervised their children and did their thinking for them. They constantly tried to teach things—with or without their children's interest. They were *managers* rather than *consul-*

tants. Their children were long on fear and timidness, short on initiative, confidence, and self-reliance.

The "A" mothers organized and designed stimulating, open environments for children, with a rich variety of toys and household objects. Nothing was off-limits or "no-no." Dangerous things were removed, and the child was free.

The "C" mothers actually spent more time with children, had fewer other interests, but their time was spent *managing* the child, force-teaching him, programming him. The "C" children were spoiled. They saw little fulfillment and excitement in the adulthood their mothers mirrored. They did not learn to struggle, to solve problems, to decide, or to take initiative.

Perhaps the saddest part of the study is that the "C" mothers thought they were doing so well. They were conscientious, diligent, and sacrificing. They thought they were putting their child's welfare above their own. The "A" mothers, consciously or subconsciously, realized that children have the joy of interest and curiosity and that the gift is best cultivated by encouraging initiative, by giving freedom, and by answering and teaching primarily when questions come.

The "A" mothers seemed to realize that ten minutes with a child when he asks, when he wants the time, may be more valuable than several hours when the parent has the time but the child is not interested.

D. *Stimulation.* A child's curiosity behaves a little like a beast of prey: as long as it finds enough food in its environment, as long as it is not starved, it continues to prowl. If a child gets enough stimulation, enough answers, enough of his parents' time when he wants that time, his interest and curiosity will flourish and grow and will continue to be the windows that open his mind to joy.

This principle applies even to very small children. As soon as babies can see, they need visual stimulation: mobiles, bright colors, moving objects to observe. Parents should show them things, talk to them, give their new eyes and ears and bodies chances to see and hear and feel widely different things.

*E. *The question game.* At dinner or some other convenient time, explain that being able to ask good questions is sometimes more important than giving right answers. Tell the children that you will give them a category and see how good a question they can think of to ask. Then name a category (anything from "clouds" or "cars" to "daddy's office"). As you play this game several times, you may want to explain to the children that there are "what," "when," "where," "who," and "how" questions.

*F. *"Interest" stories.* Read and tell stories that excite children and make them anxious to see what happened, stories with suspense, mystery, or surprise.

G. *Research.* If you have access to a good set of encyclopedias, teach children that nearly all questions have answers, that it is good to ask and fun to find. Spend time in libraries. Teach children where the various sections are, and how they can find books on particular subjects, things they can understand. Be excited when they discover something themselves.

*H. *Experiments.* Explain beforehand what you are going to do and ask the children what they *think* will happen. Then see what *does* happen.

1. You will need a ball and two balloons. Close one balloon with a rubber band so it can be easily undone. Say: "What will happen if I let go of this ball? It falls. A balloon, full of air, is like a ball; it falls too. But what happens if you drop a balloon like this?" Drop it with the neck open, pointed down, then sideways.

2. Put a drop of red food coloring in a glass of water. Watch the color spread. "Will the drop spread faster if we stir the water? Let's see. What do you think will happen if we put a drop of blue coloring in the same water? Let's find out."

3. Put some sugar in a glass of water. "Sugar is white. Do you think it will make the water turn white? What happened to the sugar? Where did it go? Let's taste it and see if the sugar is still there. Do you want to see the sugar again?" Pour some of the water in a pie tin. Let it stand in a warm place overnight. Show it to the children the next day.

4. Light a flashlight bulb with a battery. "I wonder what happens if you hold the bulb on a battery?" Hold the bulb on the top, on the side, on the bottom. "Does the light go on? No, you can't get electricity from the battery with just a bulb. What else do you need? Let's try a metal strip." Touch the end of the strip to the metal of the bulb and, flash! The light goes on! "The metal knob, the metal of the bulb, the metal strip, and the metal bottom of the battery are all connected. Now electricity can flow from the battery to the bulb."

5. Learn about air. Tape a tissue to the bottom of a glass. Invert the glass in a large glass bowl that has been filled with water. Ask, "Why doesn't the tissue get wet?" If they do not know, explain that the glass is full of air and that air takes up space. The tissue stays dry because the glass is full of air and there is no room for the water to get in. If the glass is tipped to the side, air bubbles will escape, allowing the water to get in, and the tissue will get wet.

Have the children hold their hands close to their mouths and noses to feel the air as it is exhaled.

*I. *Magic tricks.*

1. Make a pencil disappear. Hold a pencil up. Place a handkerchief over it. Say, "Abracadabra," take away the handkerchief, and the pencil is gone!

Key: As you cover the pencil, hold up your finger. Your finger holds up the handkerchief, and the pencil drops into your lap.

2. Tame an egg. Ask, "Can you make an egg stand up?" Let a couple of the children try (use a hard-boiled egg). Say, "I will tame an egg. Abracadabra, egg, stand!" You put the egg on the table, and it stands!

Key: First put a little pile of salt under the tablecloth. The egg will stand in the pile of salt.

3. The rope trick. Say, "Have you heard of the Indian Rope Trick? In India they use a rope. I will use a thread. This is much, much harder." Rub a comb on your clothing or on the carpet without letting anyone see you do it. Say, "Thread, stand up!" Hold the comb over the thread. The thread jumps up. Say, "Abracadabra, thread, dance!" Move the comb and the thread moves. Of course, rubbing the comb gives it static electricity.

4. Write through your hand. Say, "I will make a mark here." Mark your palm with ink and close your hand while the ink is wet. Then mark the back of your hand. Say, "Mark, go through my hand and make a cross." Open your hand, and there is a cross on your palm!

Key: Put the first mark diagonally across the large fold extending from between your forefinger and middle finger, and it will make a cross when you close your hand.

5. Stick pins in a balloon. Show a blown-up balloon and say, "I will stick pins in this balloon, but the balloon will not

break." You stick one pin into it. Nothing happens. Stick in
another pin, and another. Three pins are in the balloon but it
does not break.

Key: Blow up the balloon before you do the trick. Put clear
plastic tape on it. Stick the pins through the tape. The tape
holds the balloon together so it does not break.

6. Penny, come and go. A clear drinking glass stands upside down on a sheet of white paper. Put a penny on the paper.
Then take a large cone (rolled from a newspaper). Cover the
glass with the cone and place the glass and the cone over the
penny. Say, "Penny, go away, abracadabra." Take off the cone
and the penny is gone! Now say, "Penny, come back." Again
cover the glass with the cone, lift off the glass (with the cone)
and there is the penny.

Key: Paste a circle of white paper over the mouth of the
glass. It will not show when the glass stands on the white
paper. The cone helps hide the paper on the glass. When you
set the glass over the penny, the paper hides the penny.

7. Milk in a hat. You put a paper cup in a hat. Then take it
out and pour milk from a pitcher into the hat. "Oh, dear," you
say. "I made a mistake! I will try again." You put the cup back
in the hat and take it right out. Surprise! The cup is full of
milk. There is no milk in the hat.

Key: Use two paper cups. Cut the rolled rim off of one. Cut
the bottom out of the other and fit that cup inside the first one.
Together they will look like one cup. Set both in the hat. Take
out only the one that has no bottom. Leave the other cup in the
hat and pour milk into it. Then set the cup without a bottom in
the full cup and lift out both together. Pour the milk back into
the pitcher. Show the inside of the hat.

J. *Early academic skills.* The direction of this book is away
from forced, early academic skills, against the idea of pushing
three- and four-year-olds to learn their basic reading and
number skills a year or two early, against using these incredible impressionable years in teaching something as ordinary as
the academic skills that they will spend the next twelve years
learning anyway.

But there is another side of the coin that cannot go un-
noticed. A child's academic confidence, which will largely determine how well he does in his twelve or more years of formal
schooling, is largely framed in his earliest school experi-

ences—kindergarten and first grade. A child who senses that he is behind, that some of his peers can read words and write numbers and he cannot, may suffer an academic self-image deflation that is hard and time-consuming to overcome. There are two fairly straightforward ways to avoid this:

1. Tell the five-year-old that some children have had early reading or writing or numbers instruction and will naturally know more at first, but not to worry because "You will soon catch up." Go a step further and tell the five-year-old that he has been busy learning other things about his body and about the earth and about other happy things that are most important. Tell him that now the time has come for school, and that he will catch up to those who started that kind of schooling earlier.

2. Three or four months before school starts, teach the five-year-old some basic school-related skills that will give him early confidence. By then he will be curious about school and will have questions that will make him attentive and anxious to learn some basic academic skills.

The following checklist represents what a child ought to be able to do before his first day of school in order to start off with confidence. Your child will already know many things on the list through the natural consequences of growing up and of being curious and asking. The others can easily be taught in the months immediately preceding school.

Shapes
   Trace shapes
   Copy shapes
   Match shapes and equal numbers of shapes
   Recognize shapes in familiar objects
   Recognize by name and be able to draw circles, squares,
      triangles, and rectangles
Colors
   Match basic colors
   Identify basic colors
   Describe colors by name
   Relate colors to familiar objects
Letters
   Trace and copy letters
   Remember order of three letters
   Connect matching letters

Match letters
Recognize letters in own name
Print own name (lowercase except first initial)

Numbers

Trace and copy numbers
Identify written numbers up to ten
Compare larger-smaller numbers by circling largest
Count to twenty
Relate groups of objects to numbers
Know phone number and street address

III. Family Focal Point: The Family Interest Book

Children who are made to feel proud of their interest and curiosity quickly want to share what they have noticed. If they have a way to share the discoveries or fruits of their curiosity and interest, that becomes an additional motivation to continue to be curious and interested.

In our family, we have an "interest book," not for finances or money, but for *interest* interest. It is nothing more than a simple, hardbound book of blank paper in which any family member can make note of something interesting that he has observed or discovered. Preschoolers, of course, dictate their observations for a grown-up to write. Reading back through that interest book is a continual joy.

"A blue and black bird is building a nest in the tree by the corner of the house." (Saren, age four.)

"Barney (our dog) can get over to his friend's house because there is a hole in the fence where it goes behind the shed." (Shawni, age three.)

"When you kick a rock so it bounces across the patio, it makes a hollow sound." (Daddy.)

"The reason robins stand so still before they peck for a worm is that they are *listening* to know where the worm is—they can hear the worm—that's why they cock their heads." (Saren, age five.)

Our interest book hangs on a hook in the family room. We are aware of it, so we like to share in it. Every month or so we read all the entries that have been made. Like certain other types of interest books, ours grows in value with the passage of time.

IV. Story: "Maisey and Daisey"

Maisey and Daisey were squirrels, and they were sisters. Maisey always hurried, while Daisey was always curious. One day they were walking to school and remembered it was their teacher's birthday. "I wish it were later in the year and the flowers were blooming," said Maisey. "We could bring her a bouquet!" "Well, there are some flowers blooming," said Daisey. "I saw them yesterday just down from the bridge over the creek." (Daisey, you see, noticed nearly everything.)

So off the girls went to the bridge. Maisey was hurrying to get there, but Daisey was noticing while they were walking. She noticed a big, hollow tree and a red ribbon someone had dropped, and she noticed that it was getting windy and cloudy.

They found the flowers and picked them. "Oh, if we only had something to hold them together," said Maisey. Daisey held up the red ribbon she had found. It was perfect. They tied the stems of the flowers together and started back for school.

Daisey was still noticing the wind and the clouds, and when they came to the big, hollow tree, she said, "Maisey, it's going to rain. If we go on, we'll get very wet. But if we get into this big, hollow tree, we can stay dry until the rain stops." It was a good idea, and that's exactly what they did.

The rain didn't last long, and they soon came out, nice and dry, with a dry bouquet of flowers and a dry ribbon. Maisey looked at her sister Daisey and said, "If it weren't for you noticing everything so well, we wouldn't have any flowers for our teacher. And even if we had flowers, we wouldn't have a ribbon. And even if we had flowers and a ribbon, they would have all been spoiled and we would have been spoiled if you hadn't noticed that tree. I'm going to try to notice things as you always do."

That made Daisey happy, and they put their arms around each other's shoulders and skipped off to school.

V. Reading List (Including Out-of-print Titles)

Allen, L. *Mr. Jolly's Sidewalk Market.* New York: Holt, Rinehart and Winston, 1968. (A story told in interest-producing pictures.)

Barlowe, D. and S. *Who Lives Here?* New York: Random House, 1980. (About animal homes.)

Bennett, R. *What Do You Think?* New York: World Publishing, 1958. (Discusses the thinking process.)

Branley, F. *What the Moon Is Like.* New York: Thomas Y. Crowell, 1968. (Part of a series of "Let's Read and Find Out" books.)

Brown, M. W. *The Noisy Book.* New York: Harper and Row, 1950. (Allows children to think about and guess the sources of different sounds.)

————. *Who Lives Here?* New York: Golden Press, 1969. (Creative ending for a simple text.)

Cook, B. *The Curious Little Kitten.* New York: Young Scott Books, 1956. (Adventures of a curious kitten.)

De Regniers, B. *It Does Not Say "Meow."* Boston: Houghton Mifflin, 1972. (Riddles about animals.)

Epstain, S. and B. *Grandpa's Wonderful Glass.* New York: Grosset and Dunlop, 1962. (A child discovers many interesting things through a magnifying glass.)

Ford, B. G. *Do You Know?* New York: Random House, 1979. (100 fascinating things to know.)

Garelick, M. *Where Does the Butterfly Go When It Rains?* New York: Scholastic Book Services, 1970. (Interesting observations with questions to think about.)

Gay, Z. *What's Your Name?* New York: Viking Press, 1955. (Simple riddles about animal friends to answer.)

Greene, C. *The Super Snoops and the Missing Sleepers.* Chicago: Childrens Press, 1976. (A simple whodunit.)

Hallinan, P. K. *Just Open a Book.* Chicago: Childrens Press, 1981. (Charming text and illustrations about the pleasures one can find in a book.)

Hayes, S. *Where Did the Baby Go?* New York: Golden Press, 1974. (Child finds baby pictures and discovers the baby is she.)

Heller, A. *Let's Take a Walk.* New York: Holt, Rinehart and Winston, 1963. (A story told with pictures that arouse curiosity.)

Hoban, R. *Herman the Loser.* New York: Harper and Row, 1961. (Others hurry on, but Herman takes time to look and explore.)

Johnston, D. *Stop, Look, and Listen.* Cincinnati: Standard Publishing, 1977. (Father helps child to be observant.)

Kalusky, R. *Is It Blue as a Butterfly?* Englewood Cliffs, New Jersey: Prentice-Hall, 1965. (A little girl asks her daddy questions to figure out what he had brought to surprise her.)

Lemke, H. *Places and Faces.* New York: Scroll Press, 1978. (Interesting pictures to explore—no text.)

Moncure, J. *What Causes It?* Chicago: Child's World, 1977. (A beginning book about weather, with simple answers.)

Odor, R. *My Wonder Book.* Chicago: Child's World, 1977. (Small things in nature that are wonderful to discover.)

Paull, G. *Freddy the Curious Cat.* New York: Doubleday, 1958. (A cat—and the reader—wonders what is in a hole.)

Poulet, V. *Blue Bug Goes to the Library.* Chicago: Childrens Press, 1979. (Blue Bug discovers the wonderful things a library can offer.)

Rand, P. *I Know a Lot of Things.* New York: Harcourt Brace Jovanovich, 1973. (Pictures and text about things a little child has already learned through curiosity.)

Raskin, E. *Nothing Ever Happens on My Block.* New York: Atheneum, 1977. (A little boy is unaware of all the interesting things that go on around him.)

Rey, H. A. *Curious George.* Boston: Houghton Mifflin, 1973. (A monkey is *too* curious and gets into trouble.)

———. *Feed the Animals.* Boston: Houghton Mifflin, 1975. (A zoo story about what the animals eat.)

Schneider, N. *While Susie Sleeps.* Reading, Massachusetts: Addison-Wesley, 1948. (About things that go on while most people are sleeping.)

Schwartz, J. *Now I Know.* New York: McGraw-Hill, 1955. (A little boy finds answers to his questions by observing and experimenting.)

Shapp, M. and C. *Let's Find Out Books.* New York: Watts, Franklin, 1975. (A series of books on subjects like babies, houses, water, and so on.)

Spier, P. *Fast-Slow, High-Low.* New York: Doubleday, 1979. (A book about opposites.)

Tobias, T. *Where Does It Come From? That's a Good Question.* Chicago: Childrens Press, 1977. (Simple, thought-provoking questions.)

Wyler, R. *Magic Secrets.* New York: Scholastic Book Services, 1971. (Simple "magic" tricks and how to do them.)

———. *What Happens If?* New York: Scholastic Book Services, 1974. (Simple science experiments a child can do.)

Teaching the Joy of Imagination and Creativity 5

If one can imagine, he can create. If he can create, he can make the world a better place. Imagination is the first spark that ignites the flame of fulfillment.

I. Examples and Description

A. *Adult:* I remember one occasion while we were dating that Linda gave me a glimpse of the joy of imagination and creativity. I called her one crisp, autumn Saturday morning to see if we could spend the day together. She said, "Sure, but let me plan what we do this time." I agreed. She said, "Come on over, and wear old clothes."

When I got there, she came out with an assortment of sketch pads, paints, and brushes. "But I can't paint," I said. "Neither can I," she said. "I borrowed these ."

Under her direction, I drove toward the mountains. It was a clear, tingling day, with the sky a deep autumn blue. We wound higher into a flame-colored canyon; the red scrub oak and yellow aspen set the steep slopes on fire and made them somehow higher, vaster, so that they towered all around and almost over us. It was like driving through a tunnel of flame, with the cool blue and gray strips of sky and road just above and just below.

We turned onto a dirt road and wound upward until we came to a deserted cabin perched among the bright leaves. We set up our easels on the big front porch. Looking down from there, I thought the hillside seemed alive, each round, yellow aspen leaf quivering and rotating in the soft breeze. She said, "Now, make believe that you are a great artist." Her eyes sparkled with interest as she prepared to imagine the same thing.

She got into it faster than I did. Her brush strokes were big and bold, as though she'd painted all her life. She said, "Imagine that we just landed here from another planet. What would we think of this earth? What would we think of the town when we drove into it?" In spite of myself, I let her talk me into the discussion. We imagined as children do. We felt the joy and abandon of letting our minds go unshackled. I did more creating that day—with brush and mind—than I can remember in years before or since, and I was a better person for it—more light, more alive, more feeling. There was a certain wonder, a certain power, a certain joy.

B. *Child:* Several years later, after marriage and family, I came in the back door one afternoon, quietly, getting home from work early. Before anyone heard me, I heard my two girls, ages five and four, in their bedroom.

"All right. I'll be the doctor if you'll be the nurse."

"Okay."

"Now if we can get Barney (the dog) to stay under these covers, then he can be the sick guy."

"Yeah, and this stick can be for the operation." (I restrained my urge to defend the poor dog.)

"We'd better put the sick guy to sleep before the operation."

"These can be the sleep pills."

"Oh, but Barney won't close his eyes. I better sing him a song—then he can stay awake and it won't hurt: Oh sick guy, sick guy, you have such a big, long tongue, we will do your operation, and you'll look better and feel better too."

Later that week, at bedtime one night, I asked the five-year-old to tell *me* a bedtime story, for a change. It was an incredible story that introduced two new animals to the earth: a "Caxton," a round animal with fur and no feet because it rolls along, and a "Sarapoo," a little animal with long ears like a bunny that has such shaggy hair that it can't see. We (Saren and I) later made an illustrated book of the story.

Children's minds are the most free, the most creative, the least bound by inhibition and tradition. Therefore, it's easy to teach them creativity and imagination. Unfortunately, it is also dangerously easy to say "That's silly," or "Grow up," or "Quit imagining things." It is an interesting paradox that the times when parents usually tell their children to be grown-up are the times when the children are having the most fun, feeling the most joy. Do we really want them to grow up, or would we do better to "grow down," to be more like they are—more free, more imaginative, less inhibited?

There is power in imagination. One who can imagine himself doing something gets that much closer to actually doing it.

There is safety in imagination. One who can imagine the future may avoid "future shock" when he gets there.

There is youth in imagination, and children should know from us, through us, that they will never get too old to imagine.

A child who imagines will become an adult who creates,

who solves problems with lateral thinking and with innovative solutions, who will see the less obvious, do the less common, find the more unusual. A child who imagines being an adult will become an adult with less pain and less adjustment. Imagination is the magic "learning tunnel" that sometimes lets us learn without actually experiencing.

Too many of us think of imagination as impractical or irrelevant. Actually, in a world where children grow up to be engineers, consultants, computer operators, and perhaps many other things that you and I haven't yet dreamed of, imagination may be the best and most practical training they could have.

Oh, how children love it when they find that their parents have imaginations! I went up to tuck the two little girls in bed one night after shoveling the snow from the front walk. I still had on my big, white furry coat, so I pulled the hood down over my face and announced myself as "Polar Bear," come from the North Pole to tell a bedtime story. Since then, Polar Bear has had to come back once a month or so—alternating with other characters made up from very slight disguises and very big imaginations.

II. Methods

A. *The old standby: liberal encouragement.* Give enormous encouragement for the slightest show of creativity—from building with blocks to drawing a picture. Watch as though a masterpiece were being unveiled.

Sometimes encouragement involves more than just words. It may involve providing reams of scratch paper for the three-year-old to make pictures on. Often we tend to think of this as a waste because that's what our parents or teachers taught us, when in reality the child is creating something on each sheet and even possibly improving just a bit by being allowed to experiment. Though I have to bit my lip as I say this, recently I scolded my four-year-old for using practically a whole roll of sticky tape to get an old piece of Christmas paper to stick to his door; but it's worth thirty-nine cents to have him feel he has really accomplished something. On closer examination, I found that he had been very meticulous and had covered every square inch of the paper with the tape.

B. *The other old standby: being a child with them.* When they imagine, we imagine. Play in the mud with them, for a change.

Don't inhibit through restricting anymore than is absolutely necessary.

*C. *Seeing in the mind*. Listen to classical music with children. Close your eyes and see whatever the music makes you see. Describe it vividly: "Horses with fine ladies and parasols, trotting on the green on a clear summer day." Ask the children to do the same.

*D. *Imagining a space ride*. Say, "Have you ever been to the moon? Would you like to go there? Would you like to go right now, today? Come on. Let's all get in our spaceships and go up to the moon and see what it's like there."

Sit on the floor with your legs out in front of you and pretend that your hands are holding the controls of the spaceship. Lean back a little, as if in a reclining seat. Encourage all the children to do the same. Ask, "Are you all in your spaceships? Do you have your seat belts buckled? Let's go!" Count down from ten to zero, and as you say, "Blast off!" pretend your hands (palm rubbing palm) are the nose of the rocket and slowly raise them high as you make a swishing noise.

The more excited you are, the more excited the children will be. Be a good pretender yourself, and the children will follow along. Pretend to go up through the clouds into the sky. Look down and see the world getting smaller and farther away. Put in some details, like, "See how little the houses look. Now we can hardly see our earth. Be careful, don't bump into any shooting stars." Then, "Look at the moon. We're getting closer; we're almost there. Let's look for a good place to land. There, that looks like a good place. Come on, let's go down."

Again put your hands in the air and slowly bring them down (with a swishing sound) and slap them on the floor as you "land on the moon." Say, "Now, don't get out yet. I'd better get out first and see if it's safe." Pretend to climb out of your spaceship and onto the moon, and with appropriate actions and words discover that the moon is *very hot*. It burns your feet. Tell the children they can get out too but to be careful because it is hot.

After they hop around a little on the "hot moon," say, "Let's get back in our spaceships and see if we can find a better place to land on the moon." Blast off again in the same manner, look for a better place, and land again. This time "discover" a different kind of surface—slippery. Continue exploring different areas of the moon by going up and coming

down. You might find a rubbery, bouncy place; a place with
big, deep holes—"Watch out or you'll fall in one"; a place with
sharp, pointy rocks. Let the children have turns to get out first
and see what it is like. Let them make their own discoveries.

*E. *Making things.*

1. Whip up soap flakes with an eggbeater. Put the mixture
on construction paper and let the children mold it, then let it
dry. Praise and compliment and ask about each creation.
(Don't insult a child by asking, "What is it?" Instead, say, "Tell
me about it.")

2. Don't buy things ready-made when you can buy kits or
make them from scratch. Think of ways to make musical instruments (rhythm blocks, scrapers) and other simple, useful
things.

3. Throw away the Tinker Toy instructions and let children figure out their own construction.

4. Make things from nature—necklaces from dandelion
stems, daisy chains, and so forth.

F. *Pretending.*

*1. Save old dresses, shoes, and hats in a box or chest for
dress-up clothes. What treasures they can be to an active imagination!

*2. Pretend that inanimate objects and body parts can
talk: food that wants to be in the tummy, toys that want to be
played with, ears that want to be washed.

3. Pretend to be little elves who come and clean up the
toys; then pretend to be the little children who are surprised to
find their room cleaned up.

4. Have imaginary friends who come to play.

*5. Dramatize children's favorite stories.

*6. Fishing. In a dishpan, a shallow box, a small wading
pool, or a tape circle on the floor, place several small "fish."
These could be cut from cardboard or construction paper, or
they could be made with "shrink art" plastic. Each fish should
have a paper clip attached to its mouth.

Tie one yard of string to a short stick or dowel, and fasten a
small magnet to the other end of the string. The children can
pretend to catch the fish as the magnet picks up the paper
clips.

G. *Solving problems.*

*1. Have a hand puppet whisper in a child's ear an indis-
tinguishable "psst, psst." Let the child decide what he thinks

the puppet said. Children will often talk with less inhibition when speaking for a puppet than when speaking for themselves.

*2. Play the "How else could we have done that?" game. Examples: How could we get a chair over here without carrying it? (Tie a rope on it and drag it.) How could we get a marble from under the sofa? (With a stick.) How could we keep the tablecloth down at a picnic on a windy day? (With rocks.) How could we carry many things at once? (In pockets, in a box.)

H. *Stories and games.*

1. Try role reversal. Let the children be the parents and put you to bed or get you to eat your dinner. They will learn a bit about adulthood and will likely perform their roles better as children in the future.

2. Let them fill in the blanks of your story, thus letting their minds chart the direction of the story.

*3. Tell them a story with a not-so-happy ending; then tell it again and let them change the ending to make it happier.

*4. Have hand puppets act out stories or situations; let the children wear the puppets.

5. Dramatization of the "The Three Bears." Help children dramatize this familiar story. Assign the parts by asking, "Who would like to be the daddy bear?" and so on. Then retell the story as the children act it out. Pause when it is time for someone to say something and give the child a chance to say the line. But if he doesn't, then you say it and go on with the story. Some of the children will likely speak their parts, but some won't.

The dramatization will be more fun with simple costumes and props. You could put an apron on the mama bear, a tie on the daddy, a cap on the baby, and a ribbon in Goldilock's hair. Set three bowls and spoons on the table (or wherever you want to pretend the table is), line up three different-sized chairs (or pretend they are different sizes), and place folded blankets on the floor for beds.

Don't give too many instructions; just tell the story and let the children follow it. If you have time you could go through it twice, if necessary, to give each child a chance to participate. If not, tell them they will be doing some other shows next time and will get a turn then.

Don't worry if the children deviate from the usual story— in fact, encourage it. Examples: When the baby bear finds his soup gone, mama bear shares some of hers with baby. When baby's chair is broken, daddy fixes it. When they find Goldilocks, baby bear invites her to his birthday party next Saturday.

6. Tell the children you left out one part of the the Three Bears story—the part about what the bears did while they were on their walk in the woods. Explain that you are going to let the children use their imaginations to decide what happened in the woods. Then use the following "fill in the blank" scene.

While the bears were walking in the woods, they saw a big _____. The little bear was surprised. He said, _____. The mama bear said _____. While they were talking they heard a noise in the tree above them. They looked up and there was a _____. The _____ could talk. It said _____. Then it came down from the tree and they all _____.

I. *Creating through the ear.*

*1. Try creative dance. Put on classical music and different kinds of other good music and let your body move the way the music wants it to.

2. Sing together in the car. Children can sing simple harmony parts early if helped properly. Especially use "joy-producing" tunes.

*3. Have a rhythm band with simple instruments and marching.

*4. Play "Once upon a time, I caught a little rhyme. I put it on the mat and it turned into a _____. I put it on my bed and it jumped up on my _____," etc.

J. *Creating through the eye.*

1. Finger paint or foot paint; let children make a creative mess.

2. Bring out crayons, tempera paints, and watercolor markers, and paint together as a family. Praise each painting as unique and good, none better than the other. Provide the medium, then let the children use their own ideas.

3. Play with clay or dough—sometimes with tools, but usually with hands only. Don't tell children what to make; let them create. Here's a quick dough recipe: Mix together in a pot 1 cup flour, 1 tablespoon oil, 1 cup water, ½ cup salt, 2 teaspoons cream of tartar, and a few drops of food coloring. Cook over medium heat, stirring constantly, until dough pulls away from the pot's sides and forms a ball. The cooking takes

only about thirty seconds. Remove from heat, and knead about ten times until dough is smooth. Store in a plastic bag. This makes a soft, smooth dough that will dry out, but not enough to make things like jewelry. If kept in a plastic bag in the refrigerator, it will stay soft for several months.

*4. Observe nature and ask children if they can find any place where nature made two things exactly the same. Compare with "sameness" and man-made things.

K. *Combining creativity and imagination* (more obviously than they are usually combined)

1. Write a simple book together. Let the child think of the story and illustrate it while you put in the words. Saddle-stitch it with staples, making it sturdy and as much like a real book as you can. Let the child develop the characters and plot. Put the child's name on the front cover as the author.

*2. Show a picture. Have a child make up a story about what's happening in the picture.

*3. Give a child varied materials: styrofoam, toothpicks, pipe cleaners, colored paper, feathers, scissors, and glue, and let him make his own creation.

*4. Produce an 8mm movie or videotape together—let the children be the producer, director, cameraman, and actors. Make anything from a role-played fairy tale to a documentary on nature, such as "Signs of Spring." Record a cassette tape for the soundtrack. Invite friends over to see the finished production.

*5. Make a "radio show" on a tape recorder. Record the sound effects, and have a moderator and characters. Invite friends over to listen to the story.

III. Family Focal Point: The Mommy-Daddy Proud Board

One Saturday, four-year-old Saren was "helping" me recarpet a room. We talked for a while as I worked; then I got involved and lost track of her for a few moments. Soon she tapped my shoulder and squealed delightedly, "Look, Dad, a boat!" She had found two sail-shaped scraps and one boat-shaped scrap and stuck them together with the carpet backing. It really did look like a sailboat, and I made a fuss over her creativity.

Then Saren wanted a special place to display her boat. Mommy dug out an old bulletin board, and we hung it in the family room with Saren's boat pinned right in the center. Within ten minutes, two-year-old Shawni had drawn two pictures and with her limited vocabulary was demanding equal billing.

That night Saren dubbed the bulletin board "The Mommy-Daddy Proud Board." It's never been off the wall since. The drawings and colorings and creations of all kinds stay up until new ones take their place, at which point they come down and go directly into the scrapbook. Children, like all artists, need appreciation and praise to fuel their creative fires.

IV. Story: "Creative Carl"

It was bedtime on Monday night. Carl was happy because his family had just finished an evening of fun together *and* because tomorrow was Joy School. Carl *loved* Joy School.

Carl's mom tucked him in bed and kissed him good night. When she was gone, he rolled over on his side and felt his head sink down into his warm, fluffy pillow. Suddenly he heard a tiny, little voice say, "Creative Carl." The voice seemed to be coming from his pillow! He lifted up his head and looked at the pillow. It looked ordinary. He couldn't hear anything. He put his ear back down on the pillow, and he heard it *again*. The tiny voice said, "Creative Carl."

Carl didn't know what "creative" meant, but he did know his name was Carl, so he said, "What?" The pillow said, "Tomorrow in Joy School, draw a picture of someone you love." Carl didn't say anything. He still couldn't believe that his pillow could talk. The pillow said, "Okay, Creative Carl?" Carl said, "Okay, but why do you call me creative? What does *creative* mean?" The pillow said, "You'll find out." And that was all the pillow would say.

The next day in Joy School Carl drew the best picture he could of his mommy. He made her head really big and her mouth red and smiley. He drew it his own way, without any help from anyone. Everyone liked the picture, especially his mommy when he brought it home for her. She said, "Oh, Carl! You are so creative." Carl said, "What is *creative*?" But his mommy was answering the phone so she didn't answer him.

That night Carl couldn't wait to go to bed. He wanted to see if his pillow would talk again. He pressed his ear right down on the pillow and sure enough, it said, "Creative Carl!" Carl said, "Yes, pillow, it's me." Pillow said, "You made something beautiful all on your own. That's what creative is! You are Creative Carl."

Carl liked being Creative Carl. He was about to fall asleep when the pillow spoke again, "Tomorrow turn on the radio, find some lively music, and dance. Let your body move every which way to the music." Carl smiled because he liked that idea. Then he went to sleep.

The next morning when his big sister was at school and his baby sister was having her nap, Carl turned on the radio and started to dance. He moved his body the way the music made him feel. His mom heard the music and came to see what was going on. She watched for a minute and then said, "Carl, you are so creative, and that looks like so much fun; I think I'll take off my shoes and dance with you." And she did!

In bed that night the pillow spoke again. Carl pressed his ear tight on the pillow so he could hear its tiny voice. "Creative Carl, today you made up your own dance to that music. That's what *creative* is—whenever you make something or do something *your own way!*" Carl patted his pillow. He said, "I'm Creative Carl. What can I do tomorrow that is creative?" "You'll find something," said the pillow. "Creative people always do." Then Carl thought he heard the pillow yawn. They were both tired. Carl went to sleep. I guess the pillow did too.

The next day Carl and his big sister were playing catch with the big, soft Nerf ball in his room. His sister threw it too high, and it went up on Carl's tall dresser and didn't come down. He couldn't reach it. His sister said she would go downstairs and get a stool to stand on. But Carl said, "Wait, I just thought of my own way to get it down." Carl went over to his bed and picked up his special pillow. He tossed it up on the dresser and it knocked the soft ball down. His sister picked it up. Then she looked up at the dresser. "Did you hear that?" she said to Carl. "What?" said Carl. "I thought I heard a voice from up where the ball was," she said. "What did it say?" asked Carl. "I'm not sure," she said, "It was just a tiny voice, but I thought it said 'Creative Carl.'"

V. Reading List (Including Out-of-print Titles)

Anglund, J. *Cowboy and His Friend*. New York: Harcourt Brace Jovanovich, 1976. (A little boy has a pretend friend.)

Barrett, P. and S. *The Circle Sarah Drew*. New York: Scroll Press, 1973. (Imagine all the things the circle might be.)

Craig, J. *A Dragon in the Clock Box*. New York: Grosset and Dunlap, 1962. (A little boy shares his experiences with his imaginary dragon.)

Davis, A. *Timothy Turtle*. New York: Harcourt Brace Jovanovich, 1972.

De Regniers, B. *A Giant Story*. New York: Harper and Row, 1953. (A little boy becomes a giant for a day.)

Edens, C. *Caretakers of Wonders*. New York: Green Tiger Press, 1981.

Ets, M. H. *Just Me*. New York: Penguin Books, 1978. (Boy pretends to be different animals.)

Freeman, D. *The Paper Party*. New York: Penguin Books, 1977. (Child goes through TV screen to a party with his favorite television characters.)

Galdone, P. *The Monkey and the Crocodile*. Boston: Houghton Mifflin, 1969. (A monkey uses creative thinking to save himself.)

Gauch, P. *Christina Katerina and the Box*. New York: Coward, McCann and Geoghegan, 1980. (Imagination makes the box into many things.)

Haas, I. *The Maggie B*. New York: Atheneum, 1975.

Hoff, S. *The Horse in Harry's Room*. New York: Harper and Row, 1970.

Johnson, C. *Harold and the Purple Crayon.* New York: Harper and Row, 1981. (A child draws the things his mind imagines.)

Klimowitz, B. *Fred, Fred, Use Your Head*. New York: Abington, 1966. (Examples of creative problem-solving.)

Lemke, H. *Places and Faces*. New York: Scroll Press, 1978. (No text used for making up stories.)

Lindgren, B. *The Wild Baby Goes to Sea*. New York: Greenwillow Press, 1983.

Lionni, L. *Frederick*. New York: Pinwheel Books, 1966. (A mouse's imagination helps cheer the other mice through the cold winter.)

——. *Swimmy*. New York: Pantheon Books, 1963. (A little fish solves a problem and saves other fish.)

Mayer, M. *There's a Nightmare in My Closet*. New York: Dial Books, 1976.

McGovern, A. *Stone Soup*. New York: Scholastic Book Services, 1971. (A young man uses creative thinking to get a good meal.)

Meeks, E. *The Curious Cow.* Chicago: Follett Publishing, 1960. (About creative problem-solving.)

Merrill, J. *Very Nice Things.* New York: Harper and Row, 1959. (About an elephant who uses creative thinking.)

Moncure, J. *A Beach in My Bedroom.* Chicago: Child's World, 1978. (A little girl imagines a trip to the beach when the actual trip is cancelled because of rain.)

Pearson, S. *Monday I Was An Alligator.* Philadelphia: J. B. Lippencott, 1979. (A little girl pretends to be a different thing each day.)

Sheer, J. *Rain Makes Applesauce.* New York: Holiday House, 1964.

Sendak, M. *Where the Wild Things Are.* New York: Harper and Row, 1963. (A boy takes an imaginary journey to the land of wild things and becomes king.)

Stevenson, J. *What's under My Bed?* New York: Greenwillow Press, 1983.

Seuss, Dr. *And to Think That I Saw It on Mulberry Street.* New York: Vanguard. (A boy imagines a fantastic parade.)

———. *McElligot's Pool.* New York: Random House, 1947. (A delightful, imaginary fishing trip.)

Any good version of "The Three Bears," "The Three Billy Goats Gruff," and "Little Black Sambo" for dramatization.

Teaching the Joy of Obedience and Decisions

"Train up a child in the way he should go: and when he is old, he will not depart from it." (Proverbs 22:6.)

I. Examples and Description

Wrong decisions avoided and right decisions made produce happiness. Many of life's decisions are made simply by the existence of law: moral law, natural law, governmental law. Obeying a law always yields a reward; breaking one inevitably produces punishment. One who knows and is committed to a law makes *in advance* decisions related to that law. Most of us have decided in advance not to jump off tall buildings because we know and respect the law of gravity. To those who know and accept other laws, it can be equally natural to decide in advance to finish one's education or to stop and help those in need.

The other decisions, the laws without a right and wrong, the decisions with many alternatives, are somewhat more difficult; yet they constitute one important aspect of our development and determine in large measure the happiness of our future lives.

The joy of obedience and of correct decisions is the joy of progress, of being on the right course. Some might say that this "course-keeping" joy is the prerequisite to all other joys.

A. *Adult:* I have a good friend who likes to talk about decisions. He says: "Laws make so many of our decisions for us. They tell us what to do. When there is no law involved, there is the fun of analyzing the alternatives."

This friend relishes decisions. He loves to lay out the alternatives, to think things through, to get advice and then to decide. I see two consistent joys in him: the joy of obedience (in the instances when laws apply) and the joy of decisions (in nonlaw situations where analysis and advice can be applied).

I asked my friend once where he learned to think as he does. He said, "As a child in family discussions and in private talks with my father."

B. *Child:* Romping out of the candy store, our four-year-old Saren, just learning to count money, discovered she had been given change for fifty cents rather than a quarter. Initial excitement: "I've got more money than when I came, *and* the candy." Then conscience: "I'd better give it back to the man." Then the real joy as she came back out of the store: "Daddy, he said he wishes everyone was honest like me!" There is true joy in simple, voluntary obedience to moral law.

That story reminds me of another time, another store, another child—Saren's father. I was eight years old and buying my first bicycle. I had twenty-five dollars, saved up from Grandma's gifts and from collecting and returning coat hangers and pop bottles. In the store were two used bikes for twenty-five dollars, one a red Schwinn and one a silver Silverchief. I couldn't choose. First I wanted one, then the other. My wise father took me back out to the car, found a large, white sheet of paper, and drew a line down the center. "Let's list the reasons for the red bike in one column and the reasons for the silver bike in the other," he said. I did. I remember the thrill of thinking in a way I had never thought before. When the list was done, the silver bike was selected. (After all, no one else had one like it.) I kept that bike for ten years, and the memory of the joy of deciding on it never dimmed.

There is tremendous joy and satisfaction in learning that things are governed by laws. Psychologists tell us that small children usually believe that their desires control circumstances and cause things to happen. The time when a three- or four-year-old realizes that this is not the case, that things happen independently of his wants, can be very traumatic. Or, if he is being taught about laws in a positive, constructive way, it can be a time of real awakening joy.

Obedience to law actually gives freedom by rescuing us from the natural consequences and confinements of broken laws. Children, even small ones, can grasp these truths— sometimes more easily than adults can. Children need to be given the latitude to make their own decisions. They will make some wrong ones, but will learn, with our help, from the consequences. While they are young, the decisions and their consequences will not be weighty enough to do permanent damage. And by the time decisions become important, they will know how to make them.

II. Methods

A. *Teach children to distinguish between situations governed by law and those governed by decision.*

*1. The law or decision game: Describe various situations (or draw simple pictures) and ask with each one, "Is there a law, or do we decide?"

—Car going past speed limit sign (law of society)
—Person walking by a cliff (nature's law of gravity)
—Child getting dressed (we decide which shirt)
—Man robbing a bank (moral law or law of society)
—Child buying ice cream at 31-flavor store (we decide)
*2. Make up stories that ask "What should he do?" (Is there a law that tells him, or does he make a decision?)

3. Tell a story about a home without any rules. What happens? Is the family happy? (The story could also be about a school without rules.)

*4. Present puppet shows on rules and decisions. Any simple hand puppets will do, even if they are not exactly representative of the characters needed. The children can use their imaginations. For a puppet stage you can use the back of a sofa or large chair, with you kneeling behind it, or kneel behind a blanket stretched between the backs of two kitchen chairs. The children will be able to see your face, but you should tell them to pretend that they can't see you. You need to be able to see them so that you can respond to their reactions.

You will talk for all the characters (one in each hand) and also make necessary explanations as you go along. The puppet who is speaking should be moving while the other one is still. This will make it easier for the children to follow the story.

Don't worry about your dramatic ability. No matter how amateurish the show is, the children will probably love it and will give their rapt attention. There should be two parts to each show—the first part with an unhappy ending, as the puppet disobeys a rule or makes a bad decision, and the same situation repeated but with a happy ending, as the puppet obeys the rule or makes a good decision. Each show should be short. You can dramatize three or four situations (each with both endings) in about ten minutes. Following are some samples.

a. A girl wants to wear her new dress instead of her long pants to preschool, even though the weather is cold. First ending: She discovers that her long tights are dirty, but she decides to wear the dress anyway. At school she is happy when her friends compliment her on the pretty dress, but she realizes that she has made a bad decision when they go outside to play and her legs are so cold that she has to go back in and just watch the other children from inside. Second ending: She decides to wear her long pants and save the dress to wear on a warmer day. (Tell the children to pretend now that she has pants on.) Of course, she realizes she made a good decision when she goes out to play.

Characters needed: A mother to talk with the girl in the first part and another child to compliment her on her dress.

b. A boy is told that his daddy is coming home from work early to take him to the circus. Mother says that he must clean his room before he can go. He says, "Do I have to do it right now?" His mother says, "No, but it must be done before you go." First ending: He decides to watch just one more cartoon before cleaning his room, but he gets too interested in the television and forgets about it. When his father comes home there is just barely time to get to the circus, and since his room isn't clean he can't go. He wishes he had made a better decision. Second ending: He decides to clean his room first and then watch television until his daddy comes home.

Characters needed: A boy, mother, and father.

c. A girl finds a book of matches on the sidewalk. She knows her parents made a rule that she must never play with matches. First ending: She considers taking them home to her mother but decides to strike just one. She is delighted that it works and gets so interested in watching it burn that she doesn't blow it out in time, and it burns her finger. She runs home to mother, who treats her burn and comforts her. Mother is disappointed that she broke the rule but doesn't punish her, explaining that she already had her punishment by being burned. Second ending: The little girl decides to take the matches home to mother. Mother praises her for obeying the rule.

Characters needed: Girl and mother.

d. A boy is walking home from school with a friend who asks him to come into her house and play for a while. He knows the rule is that he must go straight home from school and ask his mother or father before going to a friend's house. First ending: His friend says, "You can call your mom on our phone." He goes in to do this, but the line is busy, and while he is waiting he gets interested in his friend's new game and forgets about calling his mother. After about an hour he suddenly remembers. He knows he has broken a rule, and he hurries home to find his daddy very upset. Daddy says he and mother were very worried about him. They love him, and they must punish him to help him remember to obey the rule. He is not allowed to have his friend over or go to his friend's house for a week. Second ending: The little boy says, "I'll go home first and ask my mom or dad, and if I can I'll be right back." His daddy gives permission and praises him for remembering and obeying the rule.

Characters needed: Boy, girl, and daddy.

B. *Expect and demand "perfect obedience."* Teach children that "perfect obedience" means to say, "Yes, Mommy" or "Yes, Daddy" and to obey immediately whenever they are told to do or not to do something. This may seem arbitrary or militaristic, but children inherently love discipline—it gives them a feeling of security that is otherwise unavailable. Always say "please" to children so that they feel your respect and love. Make "please" a trigger word by teaching them that whenever they hear it, they should say, "Yes, Mommy" and obey. When they do not respond quickly, just say the words "perfect obedience" to remind them to say "Yes, Mommy."

Children should know that they have the right to ask why, but that perfect obedience (with the "Yes, Mommy") is expected right after the why answer is given.

C. *Design frequent opportunities to make decisions.*

1. Have two kinds or colors of juice to choose from.

2. Let the children draw pictures, choosing only three colors to use.

*3. Let the children choose only one tool to work with in sculpting clay or whipped soap flakes.

4. Let the children choose the bedtime story.

*5. Set up a treasure hunt where a series of correct decisions leads to a surprise or treasure.

6. Let the children choose what clothes to wear. Help them think it through: "Is it warm?" "Will I get dirty today?"

7. Let the children choose what to spend their nickel or dime on—or whether to save it.

8. Make family decisions in a family council. (What kind of tree should we plant in the front yard? What should we do this Saturday?)

D. *Tell stories about wise or foolish decisions you have made and what the consequences were.*

E. *Reinforce and discuss the consequences of decisions.* "What will happen if you do that?" "Will that make your sister happy or sad?"

F. *Discipline*. Parents must make their own decisions about the methods of discipline, but certain principles always apply.

1. Children should be disciplined in private rather than in public.

2. Children will repeat the activities that attract the greatest attention. The key, therefore, is to give more attention for doing something right than for doing something wrong. Give lavish, open praise for the right, and quiet, automatic discipline for the wrong.

3. Children should know the reasons for the laws they are expected to keep and should think of obedience in terms of observing laws, not in terms of obeying people.

4. Children find great security in consistent, predictable discipline.

5. Discipline should be thought of as a way of teaching truth.

6. Punishments should be administered only when laws are broken. When children make wrong decisions in areas not governed by law, their punishment should come through the natural consequences of those wrong choices. (If a child forgets his coat, he gets cold and needs no other punishment.)

G. *Teach the principle of apologizing*. Children should learn that through genuine apology they can avoid punishment. Teach children the beauty of saying they are sorry to each other. We have learned in our family that when one child teases or hurts another in some way, a simple form of apology can restore good feelings much faster than punishment. We remind the guilty child, "You'd better apologize." The process for our children consists of three things: (1) a hug for the other child; (2) a request, "Will you forgive me?"; and (3) a "I'll try not to ever do that again."

*1. Hand each child a piece of white paper, a pencil, and a big eraser. Try to find erasers for them to use that are not connected to the pencils. Explain to the children that you want them to draw a picture, and if they need to erase they can change a solid line into a dotted line, or dark pencil lines into light lines, or make the line disappear altogether.

After they have had time to experiment with several drawings and erasing, conclude by telling them, *very simply*, that erasing is a little like apologizing. Say, "When you rub an eraser on a line, what happens to it?" (It is gone; it disappears.)

Then say, "When you do something bad or break a rule, what happens?" (You are sad and someone else is sad.) "But when you apologize and hug them, what happens?" (The *sad* goes away.) "So when we erase, the line goes away or disappears. When we apologize the *sad* goes away and disappears."

III. Family Focal Point: The Family Laws Chart

One of the most memorable evenings we have ever spent together as a family was the night we agreed to the "family laws." We had prepared a framed piece of heavy poster board and put a nail in the wall to hang it on, and then we explained to Saren (four) and Shawni (three) that this was to be a list of our family laws.

We talked for a moment about "nature laws" and "country laws" and, as usual, got the best definition of the word from Saren.

"What is a law, then, Saren?"

"Something that, if you keep it, you're happier, and if you don't keep it, a bad thing happens to you." The stage was now set.

"What are some laws for our family that, if we keep them, will make us happier?" The list gained momentum. Saren's openers got Shawni thinking, and the list grew:

"Don't hit other little girls."

"Don't plug in plugs."

"Don't ruin things that are not for ruining."

"Say the magic words (please, thank you, excuse me)."

We had to help with some that they didn't think of:

"Stay in bed when put there."

"Sit down in the back seat when riding in a car."

"Don't walk while holding the baby."

"Don't go into the road unless holding Mommy's or Daddy's hand."

"Mind with no backtalk." (Saren added a clarification here: "But we *can* ask why!")

We really didn't realize, at the time, what a help the list would be. Rather quickly the children grasped the idea that they were obeying laws that *they* had helped decide on, laws that would make our family happier.

Some time later, we decided as a family which punishments should go with which laws. The children decided that a little spank was the most appropriate punishment for hitting and for certain other serious or dangerous violations. They decided that "going to our room" should be the penalty for whining and for certain of the other laws. On some laws, we decided that one warning should be given before a punishment would be required. We voted on each punishment and wrote it on the "family laws board."

IV. Story: "Cheekey and the Laws"

Cheekey was a baby monkey. He lived with his sister and his mother and father in a tree. Their tree was in the jungle. In the jungle were some laws. They were called Jungle Laws. Do you know what laws are? (Things that you must do right or else you get punishment.)

Do you know what punishment is? (Something sad that happens when you break a law.)

There were two laws in Cheekey's jungle. One was that whenever you were in a tree, you had to hold on with your hand, or your foot, or your tail. What do you think the punishment was if you broke the law? (You would fall!)

The other jungle law was that if you saw a lion coming, you had to quickly climb up a tree. What do you think the punishment was if you broke that law? (You would get eaten up!)

In Cheekey's own family tree, there were two family laws. One law was that you couldn't go out of the tree without asking. Why do you think they had that law? (So Cheekey wouldn't get lost.)

Why didn't his mother and father want him to get lost? (Because they loved him.)

What do you think the punishment was if Cheekey went out of his tree without asking? (His mother gave him a little swat with her tail right on his bottom.)

Why did his mother do that? (So he wouldn't go out of the tree again.)

Why didn't she want him to do it again? (Because she loved him and didn't want him to get lost.)

The other monkey family law was to never drop your banana peels on limbs of the family tree. Why do you think they had that law? (So no one would slip on them and fall out of the tree.)

Why did the monkey family decide to have a làw like that? (Because they loved each other and didn't want anyone in their family to get hurt.)

What do you think the punishment was for breaking that law? (A little swat on the bottom.)

Why would the mother do that? (Because she loved Cheekey and wanted him to remember not to do it again.)

Now, I'm going to tell you the things that happened to Cheekey one day. Sometimes there were laws to tell him what to do, and sometimes there weren't any laws and he could decide for himself.

When Cheekey first woke up in the morning, he had to stretch and yawn, and he almost let go of the branch. Was there a law to tell him what to do? (Yes—hold on or he would fall.)

Then he looked at his two hats, a red one and a green one. Was there a law to tell him which to wear? (No, he could choose whichever one he wanted.) He chose the red one.

Then he wanted to climb down out of the tree to find a banana for breakfast. Was there a law to tell him what to do? (Yes—ask his mother so she would know where he was and he wouldn't get lost.)

He found a big banana and a little banana. Was there a law to tell him which one to choose? (No—he could choose either one he wished.) Cheekey chose the big one because he was very hungry.

While he was walking back to his tree, he saw a lion. Was there a law to tell him what to do? (Yes—climb up a tree quickly or the lion would eat him!)

Cheekey climbed up a tree. After the lion went away he went back to his own tree and wondered which limb to sit on to eat the banana. Was there a law to tell him where to sit? (No—he could choose any limb he wanted.)

When he peeled the banana, was there a law about the peel? (Yes—don't leave it on a limb.)

Cheekey had a fun, safe day. It's fun and safe when you know the laws and do what they say, and it's fun to decide things when there isn't a law about them.

V. Reading List (Including Out-of-print Titles)

Arnold, A. *The Yes and No Books.* Chicago: Reilly and Lee Books, 1970. (Everyone, even grown-ups, must obey rules.)

Barton, P. *If I Obey, I'll Be Happy All Day.* Salt Lake City: Book-craft, 1979. (The joy that comes from obedience.)

Berenstain, S. and J. *The Bear Scouts.* New York: Beginner Books, 1967. (About obeying and following good instructions.)

Beurger, J. *Obedience.* Chicago: Child's World, 1980. (Tells what obedience is, with several examples.)

Coombs, P. *Lisa and the Grompet.* New York: Lothrop, Lee and Shephard, 1970. (A little girl learns that her parents tell her what to do because they love her.)

Gunthrop, K. *Curious Maggie.* New York: Doubleday, 1968. (A little duck gets into trouble when she disobeys.)

Johnston, J. *Edie Changes Her Mind.* New York: G. P. Putnam's Sons, 1964. (Edie learns to understand and accept the "bedtime" rule.)

Lowrey, J. *The Pokey Little Puppy.* New York: Golden Press, 1973. (Puppies reap the consequences of disobedience.)

Poulet, V. *Blue Bug's Safety Book.* Chicago: Childrens Press, 1973. (Blue Bug teaches about obeying safety signs.)

Powell, M. *What to Be.* Chicago: Childrens Press, 1972. (A little girl realizes she is still too young to make the decision on what to be when she is grown.)

Reuter, M. *You Can Depend on Me.* Chicago: Childrens Press, 1980. (After letting several people down, a child realizes the importance of dependability and obedience.)

Seuss, Dr. *Hunches in Bunches.* New York: Random House, 1982. (Zany creatures plague a young boy with so many choices that he just can't seem to make up his mind.)

Tester, S. *Magic Monsters Learn about Safety.* Chicago: Child's World, 1979.

Waber, B. *Ira Sleeps Over.* Boston: Houghton Mifflin, 1972. (Ira has an important decision to make and finally makes it a good one.)

Watson, N. *Amy's Spending Spree.* New York: Viking Press, 1957. (Amy has a hard time deciding how to spend her dollar.)

Williams, B. *If He's My Brother.* New York: Prentice Hall, 1980. (A child can't understand why different rules apply to his younger brother.)

Teaching
the Joy
of Order,
Priorities, and
Goal Striving

7

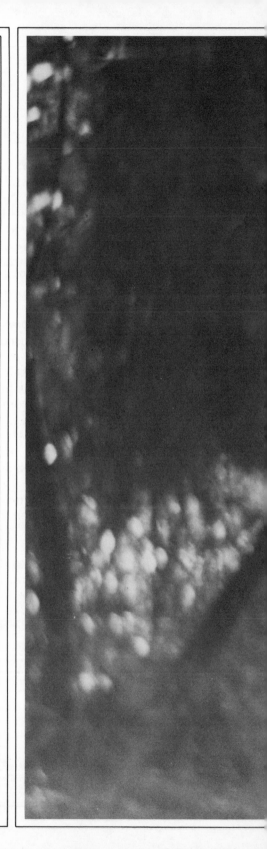

A child who can set and accomplish a simple goal will become an adult who knows the joy of changing the world.

I. Examples and Description

A. *Adult:* A speaker impressed me once with an uncommon answer to a common question. The question posed to him was: "With all you have to do, how do you look so relaxed?" (The boy who asked the question went on, partly for humor, partly for impact, to say that his father didn't have nearly as much responsibility, yet always looked frazzled and tired.) The answer was: "Each week, on a certain day at a certain time, I spend some time alone, setting goals for the week. I follow the priorities of family first, others second, myself third. I set objectives in each area, and if time is too short to do all I want to do, I put my goals into priority order so that I know the most important ones will get done. Then I plan *how*, and write my plans into my weekly calendar book."

Most anxiety comes from wondering where we should be or what we ought to be doing. Most joy comes from knowing both.

The goal-striving process sparks joy in flames of changing heat and color. First comes the anticipating, "fire-laying" joy of goal setting and planning. Next comes the growing, fulfilling, "fire-igniting" joy of hard work toward the goal. Then follows the bright, confidence-renewing, "full-fire" joy of reaching the goal, and later on, the reflective, warm embers of remembering the achievement.

Children can feel each phase of the joy. The danger is that some parents, wanting high achievers, push their children to meet their (the parents') goals and create rebellion and negative views on accomplishment, or end up with children who are high achievers for the wrong reasons. Other parents, who bring about situations in which children feel for themselves the joy of setting and reaching simple goals, end up with children who find and enjoy real success.

B. *Child:* One of my clearest childhood memories is of my ninth summer, when my dad and my little brother and I built our log cabin. I remember sights: the slow-motion fall of fir trees, the wet, white notches in the logs. I remember sounds: my father's "timburrr," the ring of hammer on nail. But most of all, I remember feelings: the good feeling of satisfied, accomplished exhaustion at the end of the day, and the buoyant joy of standing that autumn, with my brother and my dad, looking up at a finished cabin, an accomplished goal, a work of our own hands. We had set that goal, we two small boys and our father, a year before. We had drawn plans and figured where to get the logs, and Dad had told us it would be work—hard work. That experience taught the joy of having a goal, of working hard on that goal, of gradually seeing results, and of finishing and reaching the goal.

Our four-year-old came home from school one day and said, "My teacher asked if I thought I could learn these lines to take part in the school play, and I said I could."

"Well, honey, it's a pretty long part. It will be hard, but I think you can too. How can we do it?"

"You help me."

"Okay. Look at this calendar. Here is the date of the play. How many days do we have?"

"One, two, three, four, five, six."

"And how many lines on your part?"

"One, two, three, four, five, six. Hey, we can learn one line each day!"

I noticed the sparkle in her eye. She had set a progressive goal; she was pleased and proud. That night we learned the first line. It wasn't easy, but her unmodest, wide smile after she finished was pure joy.

On the second night, as we worked on the second line, she looked up and said, "Whew, Dad, this is hard, but I'll get it." (A miniature version of the joy of discipline, of work, of gradual, earned progress.) By the big day, she knew the part. She delivered it with confidence and with the joy of a goal accomplished. Her teacher has a problem now. Saren volunteers for everything, and she often says to me, "Dad, remember when we learned that part? Wasn't that fun?"

II. Methods

The joy of goal striving and achievement is like a diamond with many facets, each one a separate and distinct joy. There is the joy of knowing our long-range purpose, the joy of responsibility, the joy of discipline, the joy of hard work, the joy of planning, the joy of shorter-range goals, the joy of causes and commitment, the joy of organization and order, even the joy of failing occasionally and of sometimes making mistakes.

A. *Understanding the concept of goals.* A three- or four-year-old is capable of understanding the concept and nature of goals. Explain that a goal is "something good that we want and that we work for." Read the story "Jason and the Circus Money" at the end of this chapter. Ask and teach: What was Jason's goal? (To get enough money to buy a two-wheeled bike.) What was his plan to reach his goal? (To grow and sell tomatoes.) How did he do it? (With hard work.)

B. *Experiencing a goal.* A three- or four-year-old can experience the joy of setting and achieving a simple goal. Ask the child if he can think of a goal for himself. Help him decide on one. It might be self-improvement: learning to zip his coat, flush the toilet, or walk across the street safely. It might be solving a problem: not getting so dirty at school or not sucking his thumb anymore. It might be making a new friend or earning money to buy something special.

Write the goal down and put a big circle by it. Periodically, as the goal is achieved, let the child fill in part of the circle. (When the goal is half completed, the circle will be half filled in.)

Help the child develop a plan to meet his goal, such as asking the neighbors if they need work done, trying to zip his coat each night before he goes to bed, not kneeling down in the dirt, inviting a new child over to play, or putting his blanket away (the one he holds while sucking his thumb).

Praise the setting of the goal, praise the plan, praise every step the child takes toward the goal. Always relate your praise (or your criticism) to *what he has done,* and not to him. Instead of calling a child a good boy or a bad boy, call the thing he's done a good thing or a bad thing. Thus you reestablish your love for him as unconditional, as something that does not fluctuate with his actions.

C. *Feel the joy of setting goals and working together.* These might be anything worthwhile, from reading a book to doing the spring housecleaning together as a family. Involve the children. Write down the goal and plan it first together, go to work on it, and then discuss the results of each phase—how you are doing, how it makes you feel as each part is achieved.

1. Together, do the kinds of chores in which results are visible, such as pulling weeds, washing windows, raking leaves, or waxing the floor or car. Part of the joy comes from seeing the result.

2. Collect an assortment of cardboard boxes (from

oatmeal, soap, salt, eggs, medicine, toothpaste, and so on) and ask the children if they would like to set a goal together to build a tower three feet high (adjust this height according to the number and sizes of boxes you have assembled). With a yardstick, show them how high three feet is. Put a stick across two chairs or stools to show the height you hope to reach. Emphasize to the children that you have set a goal together to build a tower that high. Then say, "Let's go to work and see if we can reach our goal."

Lay the boxes out on the table and show the children how they can stack the boxes on top of each other to make the tower tall. Show them that a larger box should be on the bottom so the tower will stay up.

3. Reflect together on achievements after the fact: "Wasn't it great!" "Doesn't it look fine now that it is done!" "Isn't it nice to rest after getting it all finished!"

4. Have family jobs and responsibilities for each family member. For example, a little child can be in charge of clearing off the dishes after Sunday dinner. Again, lavish praise on the child, saying, "Doesn't that look nice?" Make a chart showing each family member's responsibility, and discuss these responsibilities as a family.

5. Family responsibilities can often be given to a child that relate to that particular child's gifts. Saren, whose personality has a particularly calming effect on the other children, has been designated our "family peacemaker." Shawni, with her passion for having things in place, is our "family order-keeper." Josh (mostly due to wishful thinking by his parents) is our "obedience policeman." And happy little Saydi is our "family joygiver." It is amazing how each one takes to his responsibility, reminds the others, and, most of all, becomes better at his assignment himself.

D. *Games and stories that illustrate and teach the joy of achieving.*

*1. Play games with timers. Can they do it before the buzzer?

*2. Tell stories that illustrate the joy of doing a good job and taking pride, such as "The Three Little Pigs."

E. *Teach the law of the harvest.* The joy of goal achievement and the law of the harvest are "Siamese twins"—they are inseparable. There is security in knowing you will reap what you plant. Teach this joy by actually sowing and actually reaping.

1. Have a garden. Let the children plant, weed, water, and harvest. Then use the example of the garden as a way to explain many things: how brushing the teeth grows up into the joy of no cavities, how kind deeds grow up into the joy of happy feelings, how selfish deeds grow up like weeds to choke the family.

2. Teach children to save. We have a family bank that consists of a box with a lock on it. Each child has a bank book, kept in a special drawer for safety so it won't be lost. In the bank book, the banker (Daddy) records and initials all deposits or withdrawals and pays interest at the end of each month. Children learn number skills, but more importantly, they learn the joy and satisfaction that come from saving and seeing money grow.

G. *Organization and order*. Have a good set of shelves in a child's room. Help him organize his possessions, with a place for each item. Then give strong encouragement and praise as he keeps things in their places. The simple lessons of order in a child's life will go a long way in building the critical, later-life skill of organizing his thoughts and ideas.

1. Teach a child to put one toy away before taking the next toy out. Explain that this way he will know where his things are and will not have to play in a cluttered room.

2. Gather the children in the middle of the room on the floor and tell them you want to see if they know what two words mean. The first word is *mess*. Ask them what it means. Then talk about how unpleasant it is when things are messy and how easy it is to lose things when there is a mess.

Then tell them that the next word is *order*. Explain to them that order is when there is no mess. Things are in their places, nothing is lost, everything is neat and clean and tidy. Talk for a while about how nice order is and how bad mess is.

Then tell the children you are going to tell them a secret about order. It is an important secret, and they should remember it. Get them to lean very close so they can hear you whisper. Then say, "Things will always stay in order if you take only one plaything at a time and put it back in its place *before* you take another out." Repeat this a couple of times.

3. "The Gunny Bag": Get a large bag (such as an old mail sack or a big plastic bag) that "lives" in some out-of-the-way place like the basement or the attic. Paint or draw a face on it and introduce it to the children as "The Gunny Bag" who

comes around when we least expect it and "eats up" all toys that are left out. He then returns to his cave. On Saturday he comes and coughs them up, but if he eats the same thing twice he may never give it back. He cries and cries when he can't find anything to eat.

Children will love making the "Gunny Bag" cry, and will be more aware, since he can come at any moment, of keeping things orderly and putting one thing away before taking something else out.

H. *The joy of mistakes and failure.* Discuss your own failures. Show your children that you are not perfect, but that you accept your failings and try to learn from them. The key here is simple: praise them as much when they fail as when they succeed. Praise the try, not the result. Praise the effort and show how it might be tried again more successfully. Always encourage trial and error. Set the example by being both a good loser and a good winner. And finally, tell and show how some goals take a great deal of time and effort before they can be achieved.

I. *Share some of your goals with your children.* The fact that you are reading this book probably indicates that you have a goal of being a better parent. Why not share that goal with your children? Tell them that your goal is to be the best daddy or mommy, and that you need their help on your goal, that you want them to tell you how you can improve. (It's an interesting experience to have a four-year-old tell you you've got to stop getting mad at the lawn mower.) This process of asking will teach children, by example, that it is good to seek others' help, that asking for help is not weakness, but intelligence. Then, later on, *they* will ask *you*.

III. Family Focal Point: Goal-Setting Sessions

For many years I have had the habit of isolating one hour each Sunday to set goals and make plans for the week ahead. One week, four-year-old Saren interrupted: "What are you doing in here, Daddy?" I contained the "go back out and play" instinct and told her I was setting goals. "What are goals?" I simplified: "Things you want to try really hard to do." "Can I have a goal?" "Sure. What do you want to try hard to do?" "Skip rope." "Okay, Saren. You sit here and draw a picture of yourself skipping rope. That will show your goal." It was the beginning of a tradition at our house. Every Sunday now, each family member over three either draws or writes his goal, putting a circle by it to color in when he meets the goal. We call this our "Sunday session." Then, the next night at dinner time, we take a moment to discuss the goals, to praise, to encourage, and to talk about how past goals have been met. A child's Sunday session time can also be an opportunity to think about the week ahead and to help him understand a calendar so he can look forward to events of the week and plan which days he will work on his goal. It is also a time when I can have a brief visit with each child as he tells me his goals and as I focus on him individually and make him feel important through my interest and my praise. The children have taken to using this weekly interview as a time to tell me of the private problems or worries they have.

IV. Story: "Jason and the Circus Money"

It was Saturday morning, and Jason was watching television. Between two shows there was a commercial about the circus. On the screen were elephants and dancing bears and clowns. A voice said, "The circus will be in your town in two weeks! Don't miss it!"

Jason ran to tell his mother he couldn't miss the circus. His mother said, "Jason, we've just spent a lot of money on your birthday. If you want to go to that circus, you'll have to earn enough money to buy your own ticket."

Jason thought hard about that—so hard that he didn't even watch the rest of the television show. He looked under all the cushions on the couch and chairs and found two dimes. He went and asked his mother how much a ticket cost. She said, "Two dollars." "How many dimes is that?" asked Jason. "Twenty," said his mother. "As many as all of your fingers and all your toes." "I've got two already," Jason said, holding up his dimes. His mother smiled at him and took his hand. "Come with me," she said.

Jason's mother got a large sheet of paper and drew a big, king-size "20" on it. Then she made a long tube by the side with some marks on it.

The paper looked like this:

She colored in two squares in the tube with a red crayon, like this:

Jason got the idea before she even told him. He said, "Every time I get another dime, I'll color a square until I get up to twenty!" "Right," said his mother, "and there are some old soda bottles in the basement that are worth ten cents each."

Jason found three bottles in the basement. He put them in his red wagon and pulled them around the corner to the grocery store. He got three dimes and colored in three more squares.

"What now, Mom?" Jason said. "Well, I don't know," said his mother. "Can you think of any more ways to earn some more dimes?" Jason said, "More pop bottles." His mother said, "Sorry, that's all we have." Jason said, "Maybe Mr. Johnson next door has some. I'll go see." Mr. Johnson didn't have any old pop bottles, but he did have a backyard that needed cleaning, and he told Jason he would give him two dimes to do it. Jason did it.

Jason kept thinking of things. By Saturday, do you know what his chart looked like? That's right, it was completely filled in—and it was a very good circus!

On the way home from the circus, Jason was thinking hard. He said, "Mom, do you think I could ever earn enough money to buy myself a two-wheeled bike?" "I think so," said his mother, "but it would take a long time."

That night his parents had a long talk—and got a good idea. The next morning Jason's father said, "Jason, I think if I lent you two dollars to buy some tomato plants, you could raise some tomatoes in the garden this year. If you take good care of them and sell the tomatoes when they grow, you can get enough money to give me back my two dollars and to buy your very own bike."

All summer Jason watered his plants and pulled the weeds out. When the tomatoes got red, he picked them and put them in a bucket; then he knocked on the neighbors' doors. "Would you like to buy some tomatoes?" he said. "Only a nickel each." Every day more tomatoes were red. Every day Jason sold them. By autumn Jason had sold all the tomatoes. He had enough money to pay his father the two dollars and also to buy one present for himself: a red bike, the same color as those tomatoes.

V. Reading List (Including Out-of-print Titles)

Anno, M. *Anno's Counting Book.* New York: Harper and Row, 1977.

Burton, V. *Mike Mulligan and His Steam Shovel.* Boston: Houghton Mifflin, 1967. (Mike and his steam shovel reach the goal of digging the hole for the new town hall in just one day.)

Dennis, W. *Flip.* New York: Penguin Books, 1977. (A colt achieves its goal of being able to jump the stream.)

Felt, S. *Rosa-Too-Little.* New York: Doubleday, 1950. (A little girl sets a goal to learn to write her name so she can get a library card.)

Friskey, M. *Indian Two-Feet and His Horse.* Chicago: Childrens Press, 1959. (About working toward a goal.)

Gallo, G. *The Lazy Beaver.* New York: Putnam Publishers Group, 1983.

Gehr, M. *The Littlest Circus Seal.* Chicago: Childrens Press, 1952. (His goal is to be a circus performer.)

Hall, A. *George the Gentle Giant.* New York: Golden Press, 1962. (A giant befriends children who are afraid of him.)

Keats, E. J. *Whistle for Willie.* New York: Viking Press, 1964. (A little boy tries and tries and finally learns to whistle.)

Kessler, L. *Last One in Is a Rotten Egg.* New York: Harper and Row, 1969. (A boy's goal is to learn to swim and to make the bullies at the pool obey the rules.)

Krauss, R. *The Carrot Seed.* New York: Scholastic Book Services, 1945. (A little boy doesn't give up and finally grows a carrot.)

Mathews, L. *Bunches and Bunches of Bunnies.* New York: Dodd, Meade and Co., 1978.

Moncure, J. *All by Myself.* Chicago: Child's World, 1976. (Goals preschoolers have already reached.)

Reuter, M. *You Can Depend on Me.* Chicago: Childrens Press,

1980. (A boy's goal is to develop the traits of obedience and dependability.)

Riley, S. *What Does It Mean? Success.* Chicago: Child's World, 1968. (Examples of goals that most children have striven for and achieved.)

Watson, J. *Look at Me Now.* New York: Golden Press, 1971. (What children can do now that they couldn't do as babies.)

EMOTIONAL JOYS

"All happy families resemble one another. Each unhappy family is unhappy in its own way." (Leo Tolstoy.)

In what way do all happy families resemble one another? Perhaps what Tolstoy was suggesting was that family happiness requires *certain things and cannot exist in their absence. Mutual love and respect; a mixture of independent, individual uniqueness and collective family unity and security; basic self-esteem and the confidence to try new things—perhaps qualities like these in family members are what make happy families resemble each other.*

These are emotional joys! And parents have the power to bring them forcefully into their families and into the individual lives of their small children. We can reinforce our children's natural joy of trust and confidence. We can give them the identity of being part of a secure family institution. And we can help them discover and appreciate their own unique and confidence-bringing abilities and attributes.

Preserving the Joy of Trust and the Confidence to Try

8

"The great man is he who does not lose his child's heart."
(Mencius.)

I. Examples and Description

A. *Child:* Our two-year-old Shawni came along to her older sister's dancing class. We were watching the older sister, and left the two-year-old sitting down the row of seats. I glanced over and saw her eyes growing wider. The next moment she was up, twirling, whirling, a two-year-old facsimile of modern dance. She wanted to try, to experience.

It was November, and when we got home after the dancing class it was still light and the first snow of the year was falling. Little Shawni happened to be the last one out of the car. She lagged behind in the driveway, and when I went back after her, she was sitting Indian-style in a drift, rubbing snow into her hair. Snow was new to her, and she was experiencing it in the most intimate way she could think of.

This is a joy to preserve, a joy that small children almost always have but they often lose early. (Think of the three-year-old afraid to touch the snow or the four-year-old too shy to sit on Santa's knee.) The symptoms of the loss of this joy are the phrases we have all heard: "Oh, I can't do it." "Will you help me? I'm afraid."

When did they lose it? Where do they leave it? Why? It is our fault. We fail to preserve it in three ways. First, in our preoccupations and "busyness," we fail ourselves to experience new things and to manifest the joy that comes from them. Failure no. 1: lack of example.

Second, again in our involvement with "more important things," we fail to praise and encourage their exploration. The encouragement could be verbal or, better yet, could be expressed by us learning from them, trying things with them. By criticizing instead of praising, we build fear and rub out the continuing desire to try. A child performs an important experiment by pouring his milk into his soup, and we call him a mess. A child takes off his shoes to see how the grass feels, and we tell him "that's silly," and doesn't he know he will get dirty. A child pats a big, friendly dog on the head, and we say, "Watch out, he might bite you." A child picks a flower to give to a friend, and we tell her she didn't get enough of the stem to fit in the vase. Failure no. 2: criticism instead of praise.

Third, we often compare our children with each other or with other children, thus making them feel inferior. Johnny tries to run a race or improve on the piano and glows with the joy of trying until we say, "Say, that Jones boy sure is learning fast," or "I wonder how the Smith girl got so good on the piano? She's only had lessons for as long as Johnny." A four-year-old wants to climb the monkey bars, go up a little ladder at the shallow end of the pool, or climb up on the shed in the backyard, and we say, "No, no, you'll fall and get hurt. Don't try it by yourself." Failure no. 3: discouragement by comparison or by overdone caution.

Again we've got it backward. It's children who have the joy of spontaneity, of trying new things, of trusting. We should be learning, not teaching. We should be following and encouraging their lead, not leading with our own lost ability. If we do, the joy of trust and trying can come back into our adult lives.

B. *Adult:* I spent a summer in Hawaii one year working and saving money for the next year of school. I had a friend there named Kathy. It was the first week in Hawaii for both of us. We had just met each other, and we had both just met a Hawaiian named Kiki. Kiki invited us to a beach party, "a real Hawaiian one," he said. It was on a Saturday afternoon, on a beach at the far side of the island. As I recall, the party had three distinct parts: surfing, eating, and dancing. My inclination was to watch all three. Her inclination was to do all three.

I can remember her out in the surf, trying to catch a wave, missing one, getting tipped over by the next, falling off the board until she was exhausted. What I remember is her face. Kathy was not an exceptionally pretty girl, but in that surf her face was radiant, her eyes dancing with the joy of trying something new, of feeling a new sensation. She was not embarrassed or self-conscious because she couldn't do it yet. She felt—and her face showed it—a simple, childlike joy of the moment.

Finally dark came and the huge beach bonfire was lit. It was time to eat. I had never seen poi and neither had Kathy. My instinct was to bury it while no one was looking; her instinct was to eat it and love it. I watched her expression, the corners of her mouth, for signs of distaste or of the discomfort of something foreign. Instead I saw delight—not that she had an immediate taste for poi (no one has), but she loved the experience, the new texture, the opportunity to know how it did taste. She added a little sugar and ate a whole bowlful.

Then came the dancing. There was an extra grass skirt. Right away Kathy was trying her first hula. Compared to the swaying perfection of the brown-skinned Hawaiians, Kathy was clumsy, but there was no inhibition in her clumsiness, no discomfort or embarrassment. Her smile, her sparkle, her obvious enjoyment of the moment compensated, and somehow she looked almost good at it.

The joy of trying things and of new participation and new interest is a classic and significant joy. There is so much to do in the world, so many good things to try, 360 degrees of experience. Most of us eat the same narrow 10-degree sliver of pie over and over again, too afraid or inhibited (or sophisticated?) to try the other 350 degrees. Somewhere we have lost our grasp of the joy of the basic confidence to try.

The telltale symptoms of children who are losing this joy are their words: "Oh, I'm no good at that." "You help me do it. I can't by myself." "I don't want to try it, I've never done it before." At this point we "turncoat" on them; we push them; we say, "Don't be so shy—don't be so scared—you won't get hurt—come on, at least try."

First we create the fear, the hesitancy; then we criticize it, which, of course, magnifies it and makes it worse.

There are two kinds of basic fears in the world: fear of getting hurt and fear of failure. Both kinds of fear apply to all facets of life. We fear failure physically, mentally, emotionally, and socially, and we fear being hurt physically, emotionally, and socially. Both fears are self-fulfilling. Physical fear often causes physical hurt, and fear of failing almost always causes failure.

Children are born with neither of these two fears; it is the *learning* of the fears that takes away the joy. Perhaps the easiest way to look at preserving the joy of trust and the confidence to try is to look at its synonym, "avoiding the conveyance of the fear of being hurt and the fear of failure." Remember, this is a "preserving" chapter; the parents' challenge is not to teach children, but to avoid destroying what they already have.

II. Methods

A. *Understand the delicacy of a child's confidence, of his desire to try.* In her book *Times to Remember,* Rose Kennedy speaks of the physical freedom she gave her children at Hyannis Port, Massachusetts. They could climb, explore, try new things. There were skinned knees and even broken arms—but her book correctly relates physical freedom to physical confidence, and physical confidence to every other kind of confidence (and regardless of their overall opinion of the Kennedy family, most people would agree that they did and do possess great confidence). The point is that a broken arm is better than a broken spirit. Of course, a healthy respect for real danger is important, but that is different from the overcautious fear of physical hurt that many children develop.

B. *Let children try things physically.* Break down and try things with them. Climb a tree. Jump off the diving board. It will do you good and give verbal and nonverbal encouragement to your children's physical confidence. Particularly, try things you are not good at. Let the children see that lack of skill is no reason for not trying. Lack of physical fear promotes coordination. When you think of it, athletic coordination and ability are, in large part, an absence of physical fear and inhibition.

The trick is to create a basically safe environment, rather than having to constantly warn about physical danger. Fence the creek until the children are old enough to wade in it; put the porcelain figurines up high until they are old enough not to break them.

*1. Teach small children to throw and catch soft foam balls or beanbags. Set up large pans or baskets on the floor and let them try to toss balls or beanbags into them.

*2. Fold a quilt or heavy blanket lengthwise to make a mat and let the children try various types of tumbling. Do a somersault or two yourself.

C. *Win and keep the children's trust.* The quality we call trust is basically an absence of the fear of being hurt—physically or emotionally or socially. The child who "jumps to daddy" trusts that he won't be dropped. The child who is nice to his friend trusts his friend to be nice to him. The child who returns your love trusts your love for him.

Children trust us until we violate their trust. A broken trust hurts them not only at the moment, but permanently, because it teaches fear of being hurt. Keep their trust by never lying, even a little. Don't say, "The doctor won't hurt you." Don't say you'll spank them if they do it again and then not

spank them when they do. Don't tell them to tell the telephone
caller you're not at home. Don't forget a promise. If they
never learn to doubt you on small things, then they'll never
doubt your compliments to them, your advice to them, your
love for them.

D. *Don't snap-judge your children.* Don't condemn them
without a trial, without knowledge of the facts and circumstances. We assume an arrested man is innocent until proven
guilty, but often we fail to give our children the same benefit of
the doubt.

E. *Encourage children to try new things.* Look for and set up
new experiences. When they ask for help, first say, "I'll be here
to help, but try it first." Then praise the try as much as or more
than the success.

F. *Understand the need for encouragement.* It has been said
that when we can see failure as an indispensable way of learning, we free the mind and the spirit. What a lesson! When the
basic confidence to try is replaced with the fear of failure, a
child's outgoing joy is replaced with in-turning doubt. Children, like fragile flowers, can be crushed so easily by the
fingers of criticism and comparative judgment; bright, innovative attempts can be replaced with sullen fear to try.

Parents hold the control lever. Parental encouragement
will win out over "other-people" discouragement. A "Good
try!" from parents can counterbalance scoffs from peers. It is
so important to try to avoid saying no unless real danger is involved. Instead, try saying, "Let's try it a different way," or
"Wouldn't this be better?" Substitute the positive for the negative.

G. *Praise the attempt and teach them that mistakes are okay.* To
praise the result when the result is not good violates the trust.
But to praise the try, to compliment the effort—this sort of
praise will bring about more tries and eventually more success.
We thus teach that there is such a thing as successful failure:
failure from which we learn and grow. "It's okay not to be able
to do it. It's okay to miss, to fall down, to make a mistake. This
is how we grow."

1. Use puppet shows that demonstrate this principle (see
puppet instructions on p. 80). Have hand puppets perform the following situations:

a. A girl tries to pour her own milk but tips the milk pitcher too fast and spills. Her mother says, "Don't worry; every-

body makes mistakes sometimes. Here is a cloth to clean it up." The girl wipes up the milk and then tries again to pour. This time she is careful not to tip the pitcher too fast, and she pours without spilling.

b. A boy tries to dress himself, but he gets his shirt on backward and his shoes feel funny because he put them on the wrong feet. He shows his daddy how he got dressed all by himself and says, "But I think my shirt is wrong and my shoes feel kind of funny."

His daddy praises him for doing it all by himself and tells him we all make mistakes when we are just learning. He helps the boy to turn his shirt around and shows him how to look for the tag to tell the back. He also shows him how to put his shoes side by side to tell which foot they go on. The next time, the boy gets his clothes on the right way.

c. A girl chooses a puzzle to put together. Her teacher says it is a hard one, but she thinks she can do it anyway and wants to try. After she dumps out the pieces, she finds it is too hard. She tells the teacher, "I made a mistake. This puzzle is too hard for me." The teacher says, "I'll help you. Maybe you can do it when you are a little older."

d. A boy, Sammy, doesn't want to play a new game in school (beanbag throw) because he is afraid he can't do it very well. He watches the other children for a while and it looks like fun, so he decides to try it. When the beanbag doesn't go in the hole, a little girl says, "That was a good try. I didn't get it in either." They both keep trying. Mostly they miss, but sometimes it goes in, and it is fun trying.

After the puppet show, ask the children, "Is it all right to make mistakes? Does everyone make mistakes? If we don't *try* new things, will we ever be able to do those new things?"

By *not* teaching the fear of being hurt or the fear of failure, we can help preserve children's joy of trust and the basic confidence to try. However, the two greatest keys in the safeguarding process are the two related joys that children do not inherently possess. These two joys follow in the next two chapters: "The Joy of Family Security, Identity, and Pride," and "The Joy of Individual Confidence and Uniqueness." Family security and unique individual confidence can preserve forever the joy of trust and the basic confidence to try, and can even restore the trust and confidence that some children have already lost.

III. Family Focal Point: Daddy Dates and Mommy Dates

Our four-year-old Shawni doesn't know the days of the week by name—she knows them by activity: "Church Day," "Saren Goes Back to Kindergarten Day," "Daddy Doesn't Go to Work Day." Wednesday is "Daddy Date Day." We take half an hour after work when she is in charge and when I just listen. We go where she wants, talk about what she thinks of. I encourage her as she tries things, as she says and thinks things. I reinforce her basic confidence. I watch for teaching moments that can give her the understanding that eliminates fear. Most of all, I am alone with her, learning from her the joy of trust and the basic confidence to try. What I learn from her I mirror back to her so she'll know that it is good.

IV. Story: "Sara and the Spider"

Draw a simple spider and web (using the illustration here as a guide). Fasten one end of a black thread to a doorcasing or light fixture. Thread the other end through the spider and tie it to a chair or other object so that the spider can slide up and down the thread. Then, in your own words, tell a story about Sara, a little girl who each day watches the other children play jump-the-rope at recess time. They invite her to play, but she always says, "I don't want to," because she is afraid she can't do it very well. (Explain how jump-the-rope is played—two children turn the rope while the others take turns jumping over the turning rope, trying not to trip on it.) Sometimes Sara helps to turn the rope and sometimes she even gets in the line to take a turn at jumping; but when it is her turn to jump, she is afraid to try.

At home her mother encourages her and tells her that it won't matter if she doesn't do it right and that she will never learn if she doesn't try. She decides to try the next day, but when her turn comes, she is still afraid, so she doesn't try.

After school she runs home, goes to her room, and lies down on her bed and cries and cries. As she is lying there, she looks up and sees a little spider that has fallen from his web on the ceiling. He is hanging from his silver thread.

She watches as the spider tries to climb up the thread to his web. He climbs and falls, climbs a little farther and falls again. Once he *almost* makes it, but falls again. Sara finds herself encouraging the spider: "Come on. You can do it. Keep trying."

At last the spider is almost there, and with a quick little run he makes it and is safe in his web. Sara cheers for him: "I knew you could do it." She decides if a little spider can try that hard, she can too; and the next day she *does* try to jump-the-rope. She trips on the rope the first few times, but no one laughs or makes fun of her, and she keeps trying until she can do it better and better.

(As you tell the part about the spider, move the spider up and down on the thread, moving up slowly and dropping down fast. You will find your listeners "pulling" for the spider just as Sara did.)

V. Reading List (Including Out-of-print Titles)

Anderson, C. W. *The Crooked Colt.* New York: Macmillan, 1966. (A little colt overcomes his handicap.)

Ets, M. H. *Gilberto and the Wind.* New York: Penguin Books, 1969.

Friskey, M. *Seven Diving Ducks.* Chicago: Childrens Press, 1965. (About a little duck that wasn't afraid to try new things.)

Gray, N. *It'll All Come Out in the Wash.* New York: Harper and Row, 1979. (About all the little mistakes a child makes and how they can be rectified.)

Green, M. *Is It Hard? Is It Easy?* Reading, Massachusetts: Addison-Wesley, 1960. (Things that children have learned or will soon learn to do.)

Kraus, R. *The Carrot Seed.* New York: Scholastic Book Services, 1971. (A boy plants a carrot seed and trusts that it will grow.)

MacIntyre, E. *Jane Likes Pictures.* New York: Charles Scribner's Sons, 1959. (Children try drawing and find that it is fun and that they can do it.)

Marshall, L. *Nobody Likes to Lose.* Chicago: Childrens Press, 1980. (Sandy learns about winning, losing, and trying your best.)

Mayer, M. *Just for You.* Racine, Wisconsin: Western Publishing, 1975. (A child tries to help but makes many mistakes.)

Moncure, J. *All by Myself.* Chicago: Child's World, 1976. (A child can do many things when he tries.)

———. *Courage.* Chicago: Child's World, 1981. (Examples of putting courage into action.)

Odor, R. *Growing Up*. Chicago: Child's World, 1979. (A little girl learns to do many things by herself.)

Piper, W. *The Little Engine That Could*. New York: Scholastic Book Services, 1979. (A positive attitude helps you to do things—"I think I can.")

Provensen, A. and M. *A Book of Seasons*. New York: Random House, 1978. (We can depend on the seasons to always follow in order.)

Seuss, Dr. *Green Eggs and Ham*. New York: Beginner Books, 1960. (You don't know if you like a food until you try it.)

Simon, N. *Nobody's Perfect, Not Even My Mother*. Chicago: Albert Whitman, 1981. (About making mistakes . . . everyone does sometimes.)

Wade, A. *A Promise Is for Keeping*. Chicago: Childrens Press, 1979. (About the importance of keeping promises.)

Watson, J. *Look At Me Now*. New York: Golden Press, 1971. (Things that children become old enough to do.)

Williams, G. *Timid Timothy*. Reading, Massachusetts: Addison-Wesley, 1944. (A kitten who tried and learned to be brave.)

Zolotow, C. *Over and Over*. New York: Harper and Row, 1957. (We can trust all the special days of the year to come again and again.)

Teaching
the Joy of
Family
Security,
Identity, and
Pride

9

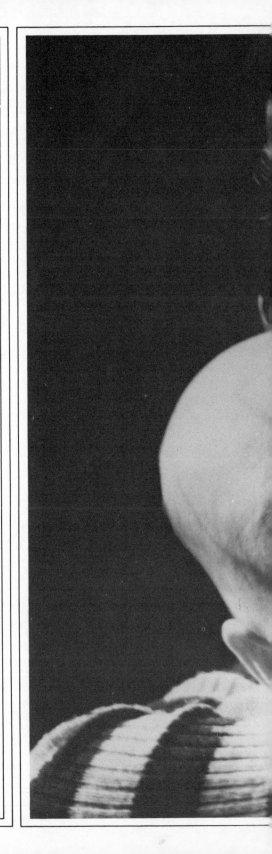

"Our home joys are the most delightful earth affords, and the joy of parents in their children is the most holy joy of humanity. It makes their hearts pure and good." (Johann Heinrich Pestalozzi.)

I. Examples and Description

A. *Adult:* When I was growing up, I knew a group of brothers and sisters, schoolmates of mine. I was always impressed because they seemed so unconcerned about being with the "in-group" or the "right people." They didn't even care much about wearing the newest thing, the latest style. They were all friendly, though, and all well liked. They seemed so secure, unafraid of failure.

Each of the six had his own personality, but all possessed one similar quality, a quality that I grew to greatly admire. It was a peace, a calm, a security, a naturalness, a confidence. None of these adjectives quite describe it, but it was there. You could feel it; you knew they had it. I was always interested in where it came from. It wasn't from individual brilliance, exceptional athletic ability, or particular handsomeness or beauty; they were pretty average in each of these categories. The clue seemed to be in their love and acceptance of each other.

I remember that one boy played on the high school basketball team. He sat on the bench most of the time, but I noticed that his brothers and sisters were always at the games, all of them—and I knew a couple of them well enough to know that they had little interest in basketball. They supported each other. Each had his own circle of friends, but none were ever too busy with friends to have time for a brother or sister.

One day an unexpected opportunity came to discover the true source of their confidence. The family moved into a house just through the block from my house. Now, instead of seeing them just in school, I saw them at home, and the secret was revealed! The confidence, the assurance, the security, the unity came from the unconditional love in their home. From the outside their home was ordinary; on the inside it was extraordinary.

I remember the youngest child, who was just turning two. The first words he ever said were "Ah, mush," a phrase often used in the family to poke fun at the frequent hugs and pats and physical affection that were shown in the home.

I was with one of the sons one day as he brought home a not-so-good school grade, a grade he hated to show his father. I wish I could describe the father's reaction. There was no anger, no belittling, no criticism—just a look that somehow said, "Son, a grade could never alter my love and respect for you; I have complete confidence in you. I just assume there is a reason for this grade, and you don't need to tell me what it is." I remember suddenly realizing that my friend's apprehension about showing the grade was not because of fear that his father would be critical or angry, but because he knew his father *wouldn't* be angry. He knew that his father loved him unconditionally and was proud of him unconditionally.

But at the same time that my friend was proud to be a part of a strong family, a family that had a tradition of doing its best, he felt bad that he had let down that tradition and that family with a poor grade. He was motivated by love, not fear; by a desire to please and be part of his great family rather than by apprehension of criticism or of anger.

Yes, I know now that the secret was in the warmth and acceptance and security of that home—a joy irreplaceable, and unavailable from any other source.

B. *Child:* I'll always remember our daughter's sentiment on the evening before Linda and I left on a week's vacation. Saren was four and was looking forward to spending the week with her grandmother. Still, she knew our family would be separated for a time, and she felt concern. She said, "Our family will be halfed."

She felt the security of family and missed that security when we weren't together. I also remember the joy in her face the night we got back together, when she said, "I'm so glad our family is back together and happy again."

Benjamin Franklin thought so much of the goodness and naturalness of marriage that he likened a single person to half a pair of scissors. Something similar, perhaps even stronger, could be said about a child without a loving, unified family. No child of any age has enough confidence or emotional independence to successfully exist as an island, untied, with nothing to cling to or be one with.

A family can be a base, a bastion of unconditional love that a child can always turn to after failure, after a disappointment, after being hurt or rebuffed or intimidated. There he can return to love, to a unit that he will always be part of, always welcome in, always important in.

II. Methods

A. *Family institution.* Security and confidence are bred from membership in institutions. A great university, a great fraternity, a great corporation—each lends strength and well-being to its members. Institutions surround people with a mother-hen-like emotional protection, giving them an identity, a pride, a thing to be a part of.

Institutions *become* institutions by virtue of traditions, which become part of the institution and part of the identity. For example, a school has school songs, a school symbol, a school mascot, school codes, school decisions, school councils, school trips, school games, and school jokes.

Now take the "school" off each thing listed and add "family," and you have a family institution. Sometimes having a family coat of arms or crest adds to this institutional feeling. Many families make their own family flags, including a motto and a slogan, and find that their small children delight in thinking of a family as something important enough and permanent enough to have its own flag.

B. *Genealogy.* Children love knowing "where they came from" in the genealogical sense. Some ways to convey this are:

1. Frame old family pictures and group them together on a special wall.

2. Tell true stories about the parents as children, including memories about grandparents. These will become the favorite bedtime stories and will get a child in touch with his roots. We know one family who took a large, hardbound ledger book and turned it into what they call their "Ancestor Book." The two parents have written stories in children's language about their parents, grandparents, and even one or two great-grandparents—simple incidents and experiences from their lives, particularly their childhoods. Best of all, the children have illustrated the stories and therefore seem to remember every detail. It has become the children's favorite storybook, and the parents claim that they see a distinct look of pride on the children's faces as they hear of the courage and good deeds of their ancestors.

3. Draw a simple family tree, with each child as a branch, the parents as the trunk, and the grandparents as individual roots. Put pictures of the parents and grandparents on the trunk and roots and of brothers and sisters on the limbs. Frame it and hang it on the same wall as the ancestor pictures.

C. *Consistency.* Children need to be able to depend on certain constants in their lives. Predictable, consistent things build security. Inconsistency breeds fear and insecurity.

There are four areas in which consistency is particularly important:

1. In discipline. If a family law is broken, the punishment or consequence should be automatic, expected, and consistent (unless an apology is quickly offered—see pp. 83-84.)

2. In example. Make yourself predictable to your children—trying to always do right in their presence, but admitting mistakes.

3. In regular schedules for certain important things such as the evening meal or a weekly family meeting.

4. In always keeping promises.

D. *Constant awareness of each other.*

1. Leave notes to each other, perhaps on the refrigerator or a special bulletin board, telling where you are and when you will be back.

2. Support each other's activities. If one participates in a school play, all attend.

3. Show love for spouse openly. As the saying goes, "The greatest thing a father can do for his children is to love their mother."

E. *Story: "Billy's Hard Week."*

Billy had a hard week, but everything turned out okay! First, on Monday, he fell off of his Big Wheel bike and scraped his arm. It started to bleed, so he ran in the house and called for his mom. She washed the scrape, put a bandage on it, and held Billy on her knee until he felt better.

The next day was Tuesday, and Billy went to the park to swing on the swings. Two girls were hanging by their knees from a bar. One of them asked Billy if he wanted to hang by his knees. Billy didn't know how. He was scared that he might fall if he tried it, so he shook his head. When he got home he looked sad, and his daddy asked him what was wrong. He said he felt bad because he couldn't hang by his knees. His daddy told him not to worry. He held him on his lap and told him how good he was at singing and at tying his own shoes. His dad said that on Saturday he would take Billy to the park and teach him to hang by his knees.

The next day was Wednesday. Billy went to play with his friends Chris and Mike. Chris and Mike were mean to Billy.

They told him that they had a club, and that Billy couldn't be in it. Billy was sad. He walked home. While he was walking he had a good thought. He remembered that his family loved him. He thought: "I'm glad I'm in my family. I belong to my family. We all love each other and help each other."

Billy couldn't wait to get home because he knew he would get a big hug and kiss from whoever saw him first. As he walked up to his front door he said, right out loud, "My family is the best club in all the world."

F. *Family song or chant: "Because We Are a Family."* In the car during a trip, or at some other appropriate time, teach children some or all of the following verses. You can put them to a simple tune ("Twinkle, Twinkle, Little Star" will work) or simply chant with a strong rhythm. For the smallest children you may want to chant a line at a time, having them repeat after you.

> Mom *always* loves me, don't you see,
> Because we are a family.
>
> When I'm scared, Dad holds me on his knee,
> Because we are a family.
>
> Who helps each other? You see, it's *we,*
> Because we are a family.
>
> We hug a lot and kiss . . . well, gee,
> It's 'cause we are a family.
>
> We work at becoming the best we can be,
> Because we are a family.
>
> We keep our house as neat as can be,
> Because we are a family.
>
> We work things out when we disagree,
> Because we are a family.
>
> My mom and dad are proud of me,
> Because we are a family.
>
> I cheer for my brother and he cheers for me,
> Because we are a family.
>
> When someone needs us, we try to see,
> Because we are a family.

We have grandpas and grandmas on a family tree,
Because we are a family.

We have traditions, my parents and me,
Because we are a family.

G. *Display open gratitude for children.* How simple—and how incredibly important—it is to let a child know how much he is wanted and needed, how precious and important he is to the family.

1. Tell the child a simple story about the day (or night) he was born and about how much you wanted him and how happy he made you.

*2. Make up a paper chain linked into a circle with a family member's name on every other link and the word *love* on the links between the names. Show how important each link is: if one comes out, no more chain.

H. *Working together.* We always do the evening dishes together. With six of us working at it, it takes only ten minutes—our record is seven and a half—and there is something about working together as a team that is fun. It leaves the whole load on no one and stimulates interesting conversation. Our six-year-old Shawni loves to repeat over and over, like a locomotive, while we're working: "Many hands make light work." It's true—and furthermore, many hands, working together, make a strong family.

III. Family Focal Point: Family Traditions

As mentioned, there is great security in belonging—to a club, a fraternity, an association, an institution, an entity with which one can identify. Children who think of their family as an institution have a powerful sense of belonging, of identity, of security. We decided years ago that we would like that identity and association to be so strong in our family that if one of our children were asked the many-option question "Who are you?" one of his first answers would be, "A member of my family."

A family should be an institution. A family should not be people grouped together for convenience, where children live until they can be on their own, any more than a great university should be a group of buildings full of books and people. Someone once defined an institution as "something with rules and traditions and pride." Certainly a family should have all three. We have talked about the first one in chapter 6. The middle one, traditions, can be the key to the third one, pride, and can provide tremendous momentary joy as well as build within children the secure feeling of being part of a great institution.

Here are a few of our family traditions, just for the sake of illustration:

1. Having a report on the day from each family member around the dinner table.

2. Enjoying "welcome the new season" family outings, such as a picnic at the start of summer or sleigh riding with the first snow.

3. Holding a special "family recital" each year in which the children sing and play for their relatives.

4. Reading books out loud to each other on Sunday.

5. Having a weekly meeting to discuss family rules, schedules, problems, and successes.

6. Sending a family Thanksgiving card to friends.

7. Making a particular birthday cake shape for each birthday: a clown cake for three-year-olds, an elephant for four-year-olds, and so on.

8. Other birthday traditions. At least one family tradition accompanies each child's birthday. In the week of Saren's July birthday we go waterskiing. On Shawni's January birthday we build a snowman and invite the neighbors over to see it, to drink hot chocolate, and to sing "Happy Birthday." On Saydi's August birthday we "float her cake," candles ablaze, on a lake and then eat it on the beach. On Jonah's April birthday we fly kites.

9. Sometimes rather small, unpretentious things become the finest traditions. We love popcorn in our family, and it is the only thing Daddy can cook. We found a special kind of popcorn in the store once and liked it so well that we bought several cases. When I took out a bottle one day, I shook it like a rhythm rattle, and little Saydi spontaneously started to dance. The other children joined in. Now, every time we have popcorn, we have to do the "popcorn dance." It's a tradition.

IV. Story: "Fluffy Needs His Family"

Once upon a time there was a baby goose. He was so soft and downy that he was called Fluffy. He had three brothers and three sisters, and every day he had swimming lessons from his beautiful mother. He and his brothers and sisters swam in a line behind their mother. Fluffy was fourth in the line. He always had three sisters in front of him and three brothers behind him. Each evening when they swam to shore, they saw their father, who was finishing an extension on the family nest.

Whenever Fluffy didn't know something, he asked his mother or father. Whenever he didn't know how to do something, they helped him. Whenever he was hungry, they caught some tasty little bugs for him to eat. Whenever he wanted to play, he played with his three brothers and three sisters. His mother made sure he was warm; his father made sure he was safe.

Fluffy learned that his last name was Honker. That was his parents' name; that was his family name. Fluffy was proud to have that name, proud to swim behind his mother, and proud to see his father able to do so much and fly so fast.

One day a big storm came, and the wind blew so hard that it made big waves on the pond. Mother Honker started to swim for shore, and the babies followed; but it was rainy and foggy and hard to see. Suddenly Fluffy saw a big wave go up in front of him. He couldn't see his mother. He couldn't see his sisters. He turned around, and he couldn't see his brothers. Fluffy was alone. Fluffy was lost.

Oh, how Fluffy cried! The storm didn't last very long, but when it was over, he couldn't see his family anywhere. It was a rather big pond and all the banks looked the same, so he didn't know which way his home might be.

Fluffy felt terrible. He was hungry and cold, and there was no one to feed him or get him warm. He was lonely, and there was no one to play with. He missed his family; he needed his family. He started to wish that he had minded his mother better and been nicer to his sisters. He started looking everywhere to see if he could see anyone he knew or anything he could remember.

Finally he saw an old ring-neck duck swimming by the shore. Fluffy didn't know him, but he had a kind face, so Fluffy swam over to him. "Can you help me? I'm lost," said Fluffy. The wise old duck squinted his eyes at him. "What's your name?" he asked. "Fluffy," said Fluffy. "Fluffy who?" said the wise old duck. "Ummm" (for just a minute Fluffy forgot his family name—then he remembered and he was so proud and so glad)—"it's Fluffy Honker," he said. "Oh," said the wise old duck, "are you the lucky boy with the beautiful mother and strong father?" "Yes," said Fluffy—he was excited now. "Are you the lucky lad with the six brothers and sisters?" "Yes, I am, sir," said Fluffy.

The wise old duck knew exactly where Fluffy lived, and he took him right home. Mr. and Mrs. Honker were very happy to see their lost baby. They put their wings around him and said over and over, "Thank goodness." Fluffy's brothers and sisters stood all around him and said, "Peep, peep, peep," in a very excited way.

It's very good to have a family!

V. Reading List (Including Out-of-print Titles)

Bannon, L. *The Best House in the World*. Boston: Houghton Mifflin, 1952. (Compares the needs of children and animals for a secure home.)

Barkowski, R. *My Home*. Racine, Wisconsin: Western Publishing, 1971. (It doesn't matter what your home looks like or where it is, as long as it is filled with people you love and who love you.)

Barnett, M. *The First Pink Light*. New York: Scholastic Book Services, 1979. (A charming story about the love between parents and child.)

Bethell, J. *Barney Beagle*. New York: Grosset and Dunlap, 1962. (About a lonely dog who finds a boy to belong to.)

Brown, M. W. *A Child's Goodnight Book*. New York: William R. Scott, 1950. (Helps a child to feel safe and secure.)

―――. *Home for a Bunny*. Racine, Wisconsin: Western Publishing, 1975. (A bunny finds a home and a companion.)

Buckley, H. *Grandfather and I*. New York: Lothrop, Lee and Shepard, 1959. (The joys of a relationship with a loving grandfather.)

Fehr, H. *This Is My Family*. New York: Holt, Rinehart and Winston, 1963. (A little boy tells about his family and his place in it.)

Freeman, D. *Corduroy*. New York: Viking Press, 1968. (A teddy bear finally gets a home and someone to love him.)

Hallinan, P. K. *We're Very Good Friends, My Brother and I*. Chicago: Childrens Press, 1973. (Some of the reasons why it's nice to have a brother for a friend.)

Hoff, S. *Chester.* New York: Harper and Row, 1961. (About a horse who wants to be loved and needed.)

Kraus, R. *Goodnight, Richard Rabbit.* New York: Simon and Schuster, 1981. (A mother rabbit calms his fears, shows and tells her love.)

————. *Leo the Late Bloomer.* New York: Thomas Crowell, 1971.

Kessler, E. and S. *The Day Daddy Stayed Home.* New York: Doubleday and Co., 1959. (It's so nice to have your daddy at home.)

Jewell, N. *The Snuggle Bunny.* New York: Harper and Row, 1972. (A bunny searches for someone to love and belong to.)

Mayer, M. *If I Had.* New York: Dial Press, 1968. (A little boy is glad to have a brother who protects him.)

Miles, B. *A House for Everyone.* New York: Alfred A. Knopf, 1958. (Everyone needs a home—animals, too.)

Moncure, J. *My Baby Brother Needs a Friend.* Chicago: Child's World, 1979. (A young girl talks about her baby brother.)

Penn, R. *Mommies Are for Loving.* New York: G. P. Putnam's Sons, 1962. (About the love and care parents give.)

Schlein, M. *The Way Mothers Are.* Chicago: Albert Whitman, 1963. (About a mother's unconditional love for her own child.)

Thayer, J. *The Outside Cat.* New York: William Morrow, 1957. (This story can easily be adapted to be about a cat that wants to belong to someone.)

Waber, B. *Ira Sleeps Over.* New York: Houghton Mifflin, 1972.

Wells, R. *Timothy Goes to School.* New York: Dial Books, 1981.

Zolotow, C. *Over and Over.* New York: Harper and Row, 1957. (We feel secure in the fact that certain days in the year will come again each year.)

————. *The Sky Was Blue.* New York: Harper and Row, 1963. (A charming story about the love between parents and child.)

————. *The Sleepy Book.* New York: Lothrop, Lee and Shepard, 1958. (Everyone needs a place to sleep . . . children feel secure in their own little beds.)

Teaching the Joy of Individual Confidence and Uniqueness 10

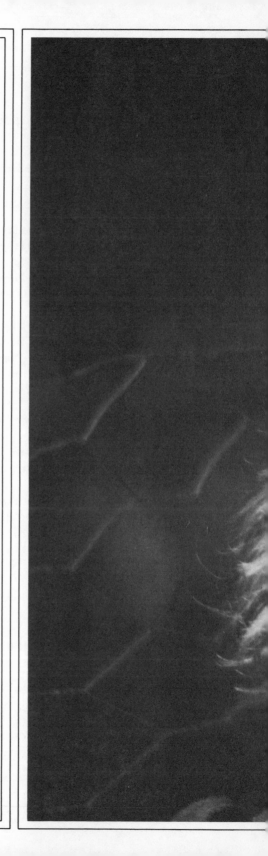

You may give them your love but not your
  thoughts,
For they have their own thoughts.
You may house their bodies but not their souls,
For their souls dwell in the house of tomorrow,
  which you cannot visit, not even in your
  dreams.
You may strive to be like them, but seek not to
  make them like you.
For life goes not backward nor tarries with
  yesterday.
You are the bows from which your children as
  living arrows are sent forth.

(*Kahlil Gibran.*)

I. Examples and Description

A. *Adult:* I have a favorite professor in graduate school, a man whose every move transmitted a certain "I'm okay, you're okay" joy to all who were around him. He had remarkable patience. When a student could not seem to grasp a point, he would not chide or criticize; instead he would compliment the student on some other point where he was strong. He supervised a research report I did, and I came to know him well. He had some strange quirks (typical, I guess, of an absent-minded professor), such as wearing two pairs of glasses at once and occasionally walking into class in midsummer with a pair of winter galoshes on his feet. He was a small man with a bad leg that had always precluded athletics. He couldn't sing or speak well. In fact, he seemed to have few particular abilities, yet he always seemed totally self-confident—not cocky or overbearing, just quietly of the belief that he could discuss anything, do anything. I guess he was a celebrity of sorts, because he was often in the company of other celebrities, from the governor of the state to the star right fielder of the Boston Red Sox. There was a joy in his confidence, a vigor, a lust for life. I'll never forget the day in class when he said that *fear* was the antonym of *confidence,* and *joy* was the synonym.

I did well in his class, in part because I found him so interesting, and by the end of the year I knew him well enough that we had lunch together once in a while. I asked the source of his confidence. To my surprise, he answered rather quickly, as though he had thought it through many times, almost rehearsed it. He said there were two elements, the first of which was his faith. He said he liked the word *faith* better than *confidence*, because faith implied the help of a higher power. He expressed to me, with no hesitation or inhibition, his belief in a higher power to whom he could pray and who he felt would guide and nudge and help him through life.

"What is the second thing?" I asked. "Well," he said, "I'm a little like the great craftsman who made the finest violins in the world. Stradivari used to say, 'God can't make a Stradivarius without Antonio Stradivari.' I have certain gifts, and I think I have discovered what most of them are. I am very, very good at conceptualizing and analyzing 'production-line bottlenecks.' I am very, very good at understanding what motivates people. I am sufficiently confident in two or three basic areas that I feel equal to anyone. I am as far superior to my friend Carl in these things as he is to me at baseball. Thus, we respect each other; we see each other as totally different equals."

I've thought a great deal about what he said. His joy was confidence. His confidence was a combination of faith and self-discovered gifts. I realized that everyone can have both, that no one is precluded from faith, and no one is without particular, unique gifts.

B. *Child:* Children can feel the joy of individual confidence and uniqueness. This fact is often illustrated by children themselves at our experimental Joy School. Early in our first year, when we were dealing with the physical joys, I had an experience that taught me something about the joy of individual confidence. A group of children were dancing, and the teacher was showing them how to skip. I was sitting at the side, observing. There were about ten children, four of whom just could not grasp the technique or coordination of skipping. It intrigued me that three of the four looked dejected, embarrassed, and upset because they couldn't do it. Each of the three, in his own way, stopped trying: one cried, one walked out, and one started acting silly and boisterous to distract attention from his failure. The fourth little boy showed absolutely no embarrassment or concern or self-consciousness for not being able to skip. He kept watching, kept trying, kept failing, kept watching, kept trying. When the exercise was over, I asked him some questions:

"Do you like to skip?"

"Yes, but I can't do it very good."

"Well, did you wish they'd stop skipping and do something you were better at?"

"No, because I want to learn how."

"Do you feel bad because you can't skip?"

"No."

"Why not?"

"Because I'm better at other things."

"Like what?"

"Mommy says I'm good at painting pictures."

"I see."

"And I'm 'specially good at keeping my baby brother happy."

"I see, Jimmy. Thanks for answering my questions."

"That's all right. Don't worry; someday I'm going to be good at skipping too."

An amazing interchange for a four-year-old! But the principle behind it is not particularly amazing—it's quite natural. A person who is secure in the knowledge that he is good at certain things can much more easily accept the things he is not good at.

II. Methods

A. *Obvious, open, unconditional love.* A child who feels an inalterable parental love has a built-in foundation for confidence. He knows that no failure, no mistake, will rob him of that love and family acceptance. Tell him of your consistent love. Always separate your anger or disappointment or criticism of the thing he has done from your unchanging love for him.

B. *Know each child well as an individual.* You can't help a child build confidence around his inherent gifts and talents unless you come to know what those gifts and talents are. Two ways to learn: (1) in private chats with the child, time spent together watching and appreciating; and (2) in organized time, spent as husband and wife, discussing each child, sharing perceptions, taking notes, discovering together more about the personality and individual character of each child. In our family, this consists of simply getting together as husband and wife (perhaps while going out to dinner) and discussing each child individually, one at a time. We ask ourselves, How is he doing physically? How is he doing mentally? Emotionally? Socially? Then we proceed through each facet for each child, asking ourselves if he is experiencing each of the thirteen joys in this book. It is remarkable how much parents can learn from each other's observations.

C. *Genuinely respect each child and his own gifts.* Our children are human beings, deserving not only our love but our respect. With this thought in mind, sometimes it becomes a bit easier to (1) show an added measure of faith in them after any kind of failure; (2) discuss our own failures with them and tell them what we learned from each; (3) praise their accomplishments lavishly and honestly, particularly accomplishments in areas where we perceive special aptitude; and (4) never criticize or tear the children down personally. We should criticize instead the bad things they have done, making sure they still know our total love for them. Never criticize in public—"praise in public, correct in private."

D. *Independence, self-reliance, responsibility at an early age.* Confidence and its joy tie directly into being able to do useful things. Each child should have a job in the family, for the family—particularly daily or weekly jobs—for which he is praised and made to feel very able and very important, very much a key part of the family.

Another way to build responsibility is to let children make their own decisions whenever possible—what to wear, what to do on Saturday morning—and then to praise their judgment.

*E. *Teaching and establishing the fact that everyone is different.*

The rock game: Blindfold the children and give them each a rock. (Use widely different sizes and shapes.) Have them feel the rocks very carefully, getting to know what their particular rocks are like. Then put the rocks in the center of the circle and take the blindfolds off. Let each child find his own rock. Teach the children that everything in nature is unique: no two rocks are the same, no two flowers, no two leaves. All people are different too. Some are good at one thing, some at another, but all are special.

F. *Help children to see what their own unique gifts are—and that these gifts are as good as anyone else's.*

*1. The "one thing I like about you" game: Sit five or six

children in a circle, with one in the middle. Let each child say something he likes about the one in the middle, such as "One thing I like about Tommy is that he can tie his own shoes."

*2. Individual profile charts: Trace a profile from each child's shadow on a poster. Then, under each profile, write in the eye color, hair color, sex, age, position in the family, and what the child is good at. Put the posters up on the wall and let each child take pride in his uniqueness.

*3. Game—"I can't do this, but I can do this." Seat the children in a circle and ask them to think of something they *can't* do, or can't do very well (they should not say it yet, but just think of it). Then ask them to think of something they *can* do well. Say, "Now let's play a little game called 'I can't do this, but I can do this.' I will take my turn first and then you can each take a turn."

You start by saying something like, "I can't whistle, but I *can* play the piano," or "I can't make very good pies, but I *can* make good bread." Your statements must be true, of course.

Then ask each child to tell something he can't and can do. If a child can't think of anything, make suggestions to him from the things you know about or from what his mother has written about him, putting emphasis on what he *can* do well.

G. *Discussions on uniqueness.*

1. Tell the children you are going to teach them a brand new word. "The word is *unique.* Can you say that? Say it again. Does anyone know what that word means?" They may guess, but it is not likely that anyone will know.

Explain that *unique* means "one of a kind." If something is unique, nothing else is exactly like it. Give some examples (each snowflake, each tree, each kitten). They may be almost alike, but not exactly alike. Something about them is different.

Say, "Is there anyone else in the whole world who is exactly like you? (No.) Then you are unique. Let me hear you say, 'I am unique.' (I am unique.) Say it again. (I am unique.) What does that mean? (It means no one else is exactly like me.)"

Then tell the children that that is what makes them so special and so important—because "you are the only one just like you."

2. Ask the children, "Which is best, brown eyes or blue eyes?" They will probably each name their own eye color. Tell them they are both just as good, but different. Ask which is

best, boys or girls? Tall or short? Three-year-olds or four-year-olds? The answer is always the same: They are both just as good, only different.

Explain to the children that they are all alike in some ways: two arms, two legs, two eyes, one nose, and so on. They all like to belong. They all need love. There are many things they all like to do. None of them likes to be hurt or sad. Say, "We are alike in some ways, but we are also different in many ways. That's what makes us special. Each one of you is special in your own way."

H. *Stories about uniqueness and talents.*

1. "Little Miss Different." "What kind of ice cream do you want?" said the teacher. "Chocolate," said one boy. "Chocolate," said all the other children except Mary. "What about you, Mary?" said the teacher. "Read me what kinds there are," said Mary. The teacher read all the kinds on the chart in the ice-cream store. Mary chose "walnut blackberry ripple."

Mary's mom called her "Little Miss Different" because she liked to do things differently than do other people.

When the other little girls wore pants to school, Mary liked to wear a dress.

When everyone got to draw a snowman in school, Mary made hers with three squares instead of three circles like all the other children.

When everyone else in her family watched television, Mary liked to read a book.

When the other children went down the snowy hill on their sleds, Mary liked to put the hood up on her parka and slide down the hill on her back with her feet up in the air.

Mary liked to try new things. That's why she was called Little Miss Different. Sometimes other children would try the same new things Mary tried, but Mary usually thought of them first. It was fun to be with Mary because she had good ideas that were different.

One warm, spring day Mary's teacher took her class to the park. All the other children played on the swings and the monkey bars, but Mary was different. She took off her shoes to feel the nice, new grass on her feet. Soon some other children saw what fun she was having, so they took off their shoes and tried it. When they had sandwiches for lunch, instead of sitting down, Mary went over by the pond and threw some little pieces of crust in the water. Little fish came up and ate them. Pretty soon some of the other children came over to try the same thing. On the way back to school everybody wanted to sit by Mary because she always noticed interesting things through the window of the car when they were traveling.

When she got home that night, she told her mom what a fun day she had had. Her mom gave her a big hug and said, "I'm glad you are Little Miss Different."

2. "Pedro the Squirrel." A whole town of squirrels lived in the trees at the top of the hill. It was a perfect place to live, with hollow trunks for houses, lovely branches and boughs for running and leaping, and plenty of sunshine. And it was far enough up the mountain that the wolves didn't come past very often. The only problem was that the nut trees were quite far away. But that was all right, for every day in the autumn all the men and boy squirrels ran to the nut trees and filled up a big box with nuts. Then they dragged the box back to the trees at the top of the hill to be stored for winter.

All the boy squirrels except Pedro helped out. Pedro was the smallest squirrel, and his legs were too short to go all the way. He tried once, but he couldn't pull hard enough to help very much. "Never you mind," his father would say. "Some squirrels are fast and have long legs, and others are strong. Each one is good at something. You are good at thinking of new ideas."

It was true. Pedro did have lots of ideas. He thought he would be an inventor when he grew up. But most of his friends thought it was better to be strong and to run fast than to be an inventor.

One day Pedro was thinking of new ideas, and he thought of the idea of putting wheels on the big box. Late that night he made two wheels and put them on the nut box. Sure enough, it was much easier to pull than before when it didn't have wheels. In fact, Pedro could pull it all by himself. Pedro was excited, but he was so tired from thinking of the wheels that he fell asleep in the box.

The next morning all the strong squirrels grabbed the ropes to drag the box to the nut tree. (They didn't even see Pedro asleep in the box.) How easily the box pulled along! Were they stronger? No—it was those round things on the bottom. Who put them there? What were they? All the excitement woke up Pedro. He popped up from the box and told the other squirrels about the wheels.

What a hero Pedro became! With the wheels, the squirrels could make six trips a day to the nut tree instead of just one. After that day, Pedro was never ashamed of being different or unique!

3. "Justin's Talent." Justin felt sad. He was listening to his sister play the piano. She was a good player. When she finished her song, their mommy and daddy clapped. Justin clapped, too. He loved his big sister, and he was glad that she could play the piano. He just wished *he* could do something really good, something that people would clap for.

Justin was four years old. His sister was six and went to first grade. Justin went to preschool on Tuesday and Thursday mornings. His teacher told the children that everyone was good at different things. Justin had been wondering what he was good at.

His mom told him that he would be good at playing the piano when he was six like his sister. Justin was glad she said that, but he wished he was good at something right now.

At preschool, Justin's friend Billy was very good at soccer. He could kick the ball hard and far. Justin was happy for Billy, but he wished *he* could do something good.

Mary Ann went to preschool too. She could draw beautiful pictures. Justin drew pictures too, but no one said very much about his pictures. Everyone clapped when they saw one of Mary Ann's pictures.

There was one little three-year-old boy in preschool. His name was Timmy. Timmy was very small and he wasn't very good at anything either. Sometimes the other kids laughed at Timmy's pictures. But Justin didn't laugh. He knew how it felt not to be good at something. He always told Timmy that he liked his picture. That made Timmy smile. Timmy didn't talk very much, but he had a sweet smile. There *was* one thing Timmy did well. He could put puzzles together. But nobody clapped for Timmy.

One day the children were playing ball. Everyone was playing but Timmy. He was sitting on the grass by himself. He had a puzzle on his lap, but he wasn't putting it together. He was watching the others play, and he looked sad.

Justin looked over from where he was playing ball and saw

Timmy. He walked over and sat down by him and said, "What's the matter?" Timmy said, "I can't play ball."

Justin put his arm around Timmy and said, "It's okay. Remember what teacher said: everyone is good at different things. You are good at doing puzzles!"

Timmy dumped the puzzle pieces on the grass and started putting them together. He looked up and his face had a happy smile. He said, "*You* are good at being a friend!"

Then Justin smiled too. He had found something he was good at. And he decided that Timmy's smile felt even better than people clapping.

*I. *Make a book about the child.* Help each child to make a book about himself. You might use wallpaper samples for decorative covers. Suggested title: *All about Me* or *I Am Special.* Suggested pages:

1. Child's name, decorated with sparkles and colors.

2. Profile or picture of child.

3. Family information, such as number of brothers and sisters and child's position in the family.

4. Personal information—age, birthdate, height, weight, eye color, hair color, best friend, favorite food, favorite color.

5. "Who loves me" list, with the last entry reading, "I love me too."

6. A handprint (made with finger paint or ink).

7. A footprint.

8. A painting by the child.

9. "Favorite things" pictures (food, toys, activities) cut from magazines and pasted in.

10. A list of things the child is good at.

*J. *Pin a badge on the child* that says "I am John and I'm special."

K. *Help each child to be secure in his own uniqueness.* Ask, "Who are you?" (The children respond with their self-perceptions— an artist, a tricycle rider, a dancer, a skipper.) "Who loves you?" (Teacher, parents, grandparents, brothers and sisters, the milkman.) The process builds a long list of reassurance and confidence.

L. *An exclusive club for each child.* Nothing makes a child feel more special than to share something with a parent that none of the other children (or the other parent) are included in. We have four such clubs in our family; each has only two members—daddy and one child. Saren and Daddy's club is "The Literary Discussion Club." (They discuss books in a very grown-up way.) Shawni and Daddy's is "The Brown Eyes Club." (They are the only ones in the family who have brown eyes. Their club has a secret handshake and password.) Josh and Daddy's is "The Train, Boat, Airplane, Race Car, and Go-cart Club." (The name is self-explanatory.) Saydi and Daddy's is "The Smile Club." (Saydi was only two when this club started, and smiling was what she did best.) There is a feeling of specialness, of uniqueness, of exclusivity, that makes children more aware of their individual worth.

M. *Special nicknames for each child.* A similar feeling of specialness comes with an affectionate nickname, especially when it is used exclusively by one parent. To Daddy, Saren is "Princess," Shawni is "Pixie," Josh is "Herkimer," Saydi is "Sugar Plum" or "Tater Tot," Jonah is "Boomer Bumpkin," Talmadge is "Mudgie," and Noah is "Nobie."

N. *Mommy and Daddy dates.* Set aside a special time each week when there is a one-to-one relationship between mother or father (or both) and one child. These occasions may sometimes take planning, and other times they may consist simply of maximizing the moment.

O. *"Empty books."* A dear friend mentioned at the time our first two children were still tiny that she got a great deal of satisfaction from buying an "empty book" (well-bound with empty pages) for each child when he was a baby and recording special events and character changes in the child's life as he grew. The ultimate plan was to present it to him on his wedding day.

We have followed her example and have found many benefits that we hadn't planned. The children know we are keeping the books and they feel a great sense of uniqueness and pride in knowing that even though, for the most part, the contents are secret until their wedding day, they themselves are individuals in their parents' eyes. They see us writing about those special events and are secretly thrilled that we take time for just *them.* Also, in reading back over events from these first few years, we realize how easily we forget those momentous moments (birth, toddler's mischief, starting school) in a child's life unless they are recorded. They'll make great "vicarious journals" and will be lots of fun for our children's children to read some day. Reading back through them is also, for us, a chance to evaluate the progress and needs of each child.

P. *A little, private chest for each child.* Give each child a wooden box with some kind of lock. Let it be his own place to keep his special private things, from ribbons to marbles, from jewelry pins to keys to wind the toy train. Then, as parents, respect the privacy of each child's chest. In our family, we made the treasure chests together from plywood in our workshop. Each child painted his own.

III. Family Focal Point: Family Experts Board

Each child has unique talents. The challenge is one of identifying them and reinforcing them. A useful tool is a "family experts board." Rule off a large mounted sheet into sixteen four-inch squares. Within each square put a picture of a family member doing something he is good at. This started in our family one night when we decided to talk about the things in which each child excelled. At first the answers were not obvious or readily apparent to us, and we realized that we didn't know our children as well as we should.

A child's age doesn't matter. We made our first family experts board when Saydi was only six months old, but she was listed as the family expert in several important categories: "noticing," "waving bye-bye," "making loud noises." As the children grew older, the board began to change; the real gifts, those things that can breed the joy of individual uniqueness and confidence, began to emerge and surface on the board. Saren, at age five, had on her list "creative dance," "playing the violin," and "being friendly to strangers." Shawni, at age four, had "singing right on tune," "sharing," "skipping," and "counting and doing sums."

Children can draw in the board's squares illustrations of each area of expertise, such as a girl playing the piano or a boy running. As parents and children focus regularly on the gifts that should be listed on the chart, they begin to identify and reinforce those qualities that give their children the lifetime gift of joy.

IV. Story: "The Ping-Pong Ball and the Christmas-Tree Bulb"

Once upon a time, at Christmastime, there were two friends. One was a Ping-Pong ball and the other was a Christmas-tree bulb. Late each night, after the people in the house went to bed, the ball and the bulb used to talk. (They could talk to each other easily because the Christmas-tree was right beside the Ping-Pong table.) Even though they were friends, they were jealous of each other. The Ping-Pong ball would say to the Christmas tree bulb: "Bulb, you are so lucky. You just hang there all day and people look at you and say how pretty you are. I spend the whole day getting hit with a paddle." The bulb would say, "You're the one who's lucky. All day you get to play with the children; they hold you and pat you and have fun with you. I just hang, hang, hang. No one ever touches me or plays with me."

On Christmas Eve, when Santa came, he had one of his magic elves with him. The elf heard what the ball and the bulb were saying. He said to them, "Would you like to change places?" They both said yes, and with one wave of his hand, the elf turned the ball into a bulb and the bulb into a ball. Just before the elf went up the chimney with Santa he said, "The only way you can change back into what you were is to get very, very wet."

At first the bulb was happy being a ball. The children picked him up and played with him—but he got dizzy from flying through the air, and soon he missed his tree branch. He wanted to be back there doing what he was supposed to do: hanging nice and still, and looking pretty.

The ball was happy for a few minutes being a bulb. He enjoyed being shiny and bright. After a while, though, he got bored. His neck hurt from hanging on the tree, and he missed the children and the paddles. He realized that he was meant to be a Ping-Pong ball; he was good at that and not good at being a bulb. Both of them were sad. They wanted to be themselves again. Soon they were both wishing that someone would throw water on them so they could change back. They got more and more sad. Finally they got so sad that they started to cry. Their tears got them wet, and suddenly they changed back into themselves.

V. Reading List (Including Out-of-print Titles)

Anglund, J. *Look Out the Window.* New York: Harcourt Brace Jovanovich, 1959. (Everyone is different . . . including his family, house, pets, etc.)

Bachman, M. *God's World of Colors.* New York: Standard Publishing, 1980. (God made things in many different colors, even people.)

Barchas, S. *Jane and the Giant*. New York: Scholastic Book Services, 1978. (Everyone has something he can do better than others.)

Behrens, J. *Who Am I?* New York: Elk Grove Press, 1958. (Short descriptions of many different children.)

Bright, R. *The Friendly Bear*. New York: Doubleday, 1957. (We are different in many ways, but we all need love.)

Brown, M. W. *The Important Book*. New York: Harper and Row, 1949. (The important thing about *you* is that "you are you.")

Charlip, R. *Hooray For Me*. New York: Scholastic Book Services, 1975. (Everyone should like himself.)

Delton, J. *Two Good Friends*. New York: Crown Publishers, 1974. (Each person has his own talents . . . we can share and help each other.)

De Regniers, B. *Everyone Is Good for Something*. Boston: Houghton Mifflin, 1982. (A boy feels like a nobody but finds out that everybody is special in their own way.)

————. *The Little Girl and Her Mother*. New York: Vanguard Press, 1979. (Though you are too little to do some things, you can do other things just because you are little.)

Disney, Walt. *The Ugly Duckling*. Racine, Wisconsin: Western Publishing, 1976.

Ets, M. H. *Just Me*. New York: Viking Press, 1965. (A little boy pretends to be several different animals but likes best to be "just me.")

Flack, M. *Ask Mister Bear*. New York: Macmillan, 1958.

Freeman, D. *Dandelion*. New York: Penguin Books, 1977. (A lion learns it is best to be your own self.)

Greene, L. *I Am Somebody*. Chicago: Childrens Press, 1980. (Nathan learns to accept his strengths and weaknesses.)

Hallinan, P. K. *I'm Glad to Be Me*. Chicago: Childrens Press, 1977. (Examines reasons to be glad that you are you.)

————. *Where's Michael?* Chicago: Childrens Press, 1978. (Michael learns that being himself is best.)

Jackson, K. and B. *The Saggy, Baggy Elephant*. New York: Golden Press, 1947. (A little elephant discovers he looks just right for an elephant.)

Kellogg, S. *Much Bigger Than Martin*. New York: Dial Press,

1976. (A little boy learns to be happy with the age and size he is.)

Kent, J. *Knee-High Nina.* New York: Doubleday, 1981. (A little girl finds it is best to be just as she is for now.)

Kraus, R. *Owliver.* New York: Windmill Books, 1974.

Kuskin, K. *Which Horse Is William?* New York: Harper and Row, 1959. (We are all different, and it is good to be that way.)

Leaf, M. *Noodle.* New York: Scholastic Book Services. (A dog decides it is best to be just as he is.)

Le Sieg, T. *Come Over to My House.* New York: Beginner Books, 1966. (Shows different races, homes, customs, around the world.)

McClure, H. *Children of the World Say "Good Morning."* New York: Harcourt Brace Jovanovich, 1963. (About different races, colors, clothes, languages.)

Moncure, J. *Wait, Says His Father.* Chicago: Child's World, 1975. (Waiting is a hard thing to do when you're in a hurry to grow up.)

Seuss, Dr. *The Sneetches and Other Stories.* New York: Random House, 1961. (The Sneetches learn that being different doesn't make you better or worse than others.) Also in this book: *Too Many Daves.* (Confusion results when everyone has the same name.)

———. *Yertle the Turtle and Other Stories.* New York: Random House, 1958. (Yertle the Turtle thinks he is better than all the others, but finds out differently.) Also includes *Gertrude McFuzz.* (Jealous Gertrude McFuzz discovers that her tail is just right for her kind of bird.)

Slobodkin, L. *Millions and Millions and Millions.* New York: Vanguard Press, 1955. (Of the millions of people, none is just like you.)

Spier, P. *People.* New York: Doubleday, 1980.

Waber, B. *You Look Ridiculous Said the Rhinocerous to the Hippopotamus.* Boston: Houghton Mifflin, 1966. (A hippopotamus learns to like himself as he is.)

Winthrop, E. *Sloppy Kisses.* New York: Macmillan, 1980.

SOCIAL JOYS

Without the social elements of life, other joys would quickly lose their flavor. Joy needs to be shared! Indeed, it is usually the parents' recognition of the need for social joys and social graces that causes them to send their small children to pre-schools. But these are not easy joys to teach, and parents should accept more of the responsibility than they abdicate to schools and other institutions.

The first challenge is to preserve the honesty and candor that all children are born with. This will help them learn the next social joy, that of effective communication and meaningful relationships, which in turn will assure their success in school, as well as their happiness there.

Finally, in the last chapter of this section and of the book, comes the most difficult as well as the most important joy, both for children and for adults. Children are simply not born with a natural inclination toward the joy of sharing and service. Once learned and experienced, however, it can make the difference between a life of self-centered unhappiness and one of self-forgetting joy.

Preserving the Joy of Realness, Honesty, and Candor

11

Because of their natural honesty and candor, small children are their true selves. If, as they grow older, they lose part of their truth, they will also lose part of who they are.

I. Examples and Description

A. *Child:* Children are born with the gift of realness, congruence, honesty, candor. At first, they know nothing else. People have to *learn* to be false, to cover up feelings, to lie. Josh just turned three and hasn't learned to do any of them yet. Last time I tried to give him a bath, the big new shampoo bottle was empty. "Did you dump it out, Josh?" His brow furrowed as he anticipated the worst, but a lie never occurred to him. "Yes, Dad." We have a family law against "dumping," and Josh knows the law, so he needed a little punishment. But I praised him so much for telling the truth that it outbalanced the punishment.

As Josh splashed in the bath, my mind went back to another time when the shampoo was dumped, when Saren was five and Shawni four. "Did you do it, Saren?" Her look showed that she was about to say, "No, Shawni did." Then a change came to her eye. "Daddy, sometimes it's hard to tell the truth, isn't it." I felt inner rejoicing. She had consciously chosen truth over a lie.

Josh pulled me back to the present. "Daddy, dry me off!" As I dried Josh, I had candor and honesty on my mind and happened to hear Saren, now six, in whom we had tried so hard to preserve that quality. She was in her bedroom with a new friend from school. They were discussing their dolls.

Saren: "This doll has a problem. Her skirt has lost its elastic, so it slips right off."

Friend: "Let's tie a string around it."

(Silence for several minutes.)

Saren: "It scares me when Miss Christie calls on me to read in school. Does it scare you?"

Friend: "A little."

Saren: "I'm getting over it, though."

Friend: "The more you do it, the easier it is."

Saren: "I guess so. There, we got the skirt almost ready."

(Pause.)

Friend: "Saren, do you like me?"

Saren: "Of course, silly. I like everything about you."

Friend: "Everything?"

Saren: "Except I didn't like it when you played with Patty at recess—but Mommy says I was just jealous."

Friend: "What's jealous?"

Saren: "Not wanting someone to have more fun than you."

Friend: "I like you too, Saren."

To be honest, to be open, to talk freely about the real feelings—what a joy!

And what a need there is to reinforce children in their natural honesty, to get across to the clean slate of their minds the fact that it is just as all right to be sad or mad as to be glad, that what really counts is being real.

Congruence, in a psychological sense, is a matching up of how you really feel, how you think you feel, and how you say you feel. Straightforward honesty and candor, added to congruence, can free and lift the mind into the clear realm, void of "games" and "fronts" and "stiff upper lips." Grown-ups, too, can find this congruence.

B. *Adult:* I watched a local political race with more than usual interest one year because my friend John was a surprise candidate. John was a surprise because he seemed so unpolitical. He was the most honest and candid man I knew, and my first thought was, "He's too honest to make the promises that win elections."

I was right about John, but wrong about the result. John was brutally honest, and he enjoyed people's surprised reaction to his unbending truthfulness. He disagreed with many of the people he was supposed to agree with. He said no to people who weren't used to hearing the word. He said "I don't know" when he didn't know.

A week before the election, John was calm and seemingly unaffected, unlike the many on-edge politicians I had known. "Don't you care if you win?" I asked him. "Maybe not," he said, "at least not in the way you mean. I've been straight on every point. If I win, the real me wins. If I lose, I'm still the real me. I'd rather be the real loser than the unreal winner." John won. I was happily surprised.

There is power in utter candor, and joy in simply saying what you really think, in being right with self and with others. The freedom of a clear conscience is endless.

II. Methods

A. *Example.* Be as real and congruent as your children are. Sharing your example (or following theirs) is the strongest possible reinforcement. Verbalize your real feelings, fears, and insecurities as well as your joys and loves. Show control, but show honesty! Tell them how you feel—"I'm upset about what happened this afternoon, so I got more angry with you than I should have." Never let them hear you lie about anything to anyone.

Forsake the forced, unnatural parental notion of not punishing when you are angry or upset. Certainly there is a need for control, but be genuine. It's all right to show some honest indignation; it is even all right for children to see a parental disagreement as long as (1) the light of love shines through, (2) it's not about them (the children), and (3) you make up afterward—and they *see* that you do.

B. *Reinforcement and praise.* Since children start with realness, congruence, and honesty, recognition and reinforcement become the two great keys. Whatever they get attention for, they'll probably do again; whatever they get praise for, they'll very likely do again; whatever they get joy and praise out of, they'll almost certainly do again. Encourage them to always tell how they feel—to tell not only you but also other family members, teachers, and friends.

Psychiatrists tell us that it's usually as hard to get a person to know *how* he really feels as it is to help him know *why* he feels that way. The reason it is so hard to know how we feel is that we stop so early in life telling anyone, even ourselves, how we really feel. We need to recognize emotions, accept them, and, if possible, enjoy them.

C. *Show acceptability of letting our feelings show.*

*1. Show pictures from magazines of children and grown-ups crying. Ask: "What made them cry?" "Is it okay?" Respond: "Sure! Crying helps to get the sad and the mad out. Just be careful not to cry without a reason."

2. Have an acceptable way for a child to show and vent his anger—a big punching bag or pillow or inflatable figure.

3. Ask often, "How did that make you feel?" Then really listen!

Oh, how children teach us! Just now as I write, five-year-old Saren has a question. I give her a too-quick, ask-it-later answer. She says, "Dad, when you say that, it makes me feel like you don't care about me. You only care about your book." I put down the book, praise her, answer her.

4. Point out mistakes others make in *not* telling what bothers them (in stories or real life or television shows). Show how it would have been better if they had told.

5. Have a pact and a family tradition to always tell the truth. Make the reward for honesty psychologically outweigh the punishment for the admitted wrong.

*6. Pantomime certain emotions, such as sadness, anger, and happiness.

*7. Game: "How Would You Feel?" You will need the bottom half of a styrofoam egg carton. Turn it upside down and cut a slit in each egg cup.

Write the following questions (or use ideas of your own) on narrow strips of paper. Fold the strips and slip one into each of the slits in the egg carton.

To play the game, each child has one or more turns to choose a question and pull it from the egg cup. The parent reads the question and the child answers it. The questions are written very briefly. You can add to them as you ask them. On the letters marked with an asterisk (*), you might also ask, "What would you do?" after the child says how he would feel.

How would you feel if:

a. You heard a loud, strange noise outside your window at night?

*b. You wanted a nickel for a gumball machine but Mother said no?

c. Daddy brought you a surprise?

*d. Little sister broke your crayons?

e. Mother said, "You were the best singer at the Halloween party"?

*f. You couldn't get your coat zipped—the zipper was stuck?

g. Daddy said, "Who wants an ice cream cone?"

h. Your mother was sick?

*i. Someone called you a bad name?

*j. You broke your mother's new lamp?

k. You had no one to play with?

*l. Your grandma gave your brother a bigger piece of cake than she gave you?

Help the children express what their emotions would be and assure them that all those emotions are natural . . . and okay.

8. Puppet shows on ways to express emotions (see puppet show instructions on page 80).

Try the following ideas. Put in your own details, speaking parts, and narration. After each emotion is expressed in a "not-so-good" way, ask the children, "Do you know a better way for Mary (or Tom) to show that she (he) is angry (or sad, or whatever)?" Then repeat the situation from the beginning with the character expressing his or her emotions in a more acceptable way.

a. *Angry*—Mary and Tom are lying on the carpet, coloring with their crayons. Tom asks to use Mary's red crayon because his is lost. He pushes too hard with it and breaks it. Mary is angry.

(1) She hits her brother and then grabs one of his crayons and breaks it to get even with him.

(2) She shouts, "Tom, that makes me so mad." Then she pounds her fists on the carpet and cries for a while.

b. *Happy*—tomorrow will be Tom's birthday. He is so happy and excited. His daddy is sitting at the table working on some important papers from his office. Tom is running and skipping through the house, singing, "Tomorrow is my birthday. Tomorrow is my birthday." His father asks him to be quiet.

(1) Tom says, "I can't. I'm just so happy." And he continues to run and sing.

(2) Tom says, "I'm sorry," and he goes outside to run and sing his song.

c. *Sad*—Mary is at the store with her mother. She sees a game she wants very much. She asks her mother to buy it for her. Her mother says, "I'm sorry, Mary, but I just don't have enough money to buy that today." Mary is very sad.

(1) She starts to cry. She cries all the way to the car. She cries all the way home, and she says, "You're not a very nice mother." This makes her mother feel bad too.

(2) She says, "Oh, Mom, I want it so much. I wish I could have it." Her face looks so sad. Mother says, "I know, dear, and I wish I could buy it for you, but I just can't today." Mary understands, and though she still feels sad, she takes her mother's hand and goes with her to the car.

d. *Frustrated*—Tom is putting together the model airplane he got for his birthday. It keeps falling apart. It just won't work the way he wants it to. He is very upset.

(1) He says, "You stupid airplane. Why won't you stay together?" Then he throws it on the floor. One wing breaks, so now the airplane is no good.

(2) He cries a little. Then he stops crying and goes to his daddy and says, "Dad, I just can't get this airplane together. I've tried and tried. I get so frustrated. Can you help me?"

9. Honesty discussion. Ask the children, "Do you know what it means to tell the truth?" Add to the children's answers, if necessary, to bring out that telling the truth means to tell things as they are: what really happened, what you really think, and how you really feel. Ask the following questions:

a. If you accidentally bumped into your mother's plant and knocked some leaves off it and then told Mother that the baby pulled them off, would that be telling the truth? (No.) What would that be? (A lie.)

b. Suppose your daddy asked you to go out and turn off the hose, but you were busy doing something else and forgot to do it. Then, if Daddy said, "Did you turn off the hose?" and you said yes, would that be telling the truth? (No, that would be a lie.)

c. If you promised your friend, "I'll give you some candy if you let me ride your bike," but you really didn't even have any candy, would you be telling the truth? (No, that would be a lie because you couldn't keep your promise.)

d. What if you took your little brother's toy away from him and made him cry? Then, if your mother said, "Why is he crying?" and you said, "I don't know," would that be the truth? (No.)

Before going on to the next situation, ask, "How do you think you would feel if you told a lie?" (Sad, bad, worried, ashamed, awful.)

e. What if _____ (name of neighbor child) invited _____ and _____ (names of other children in neighborhood) to his birthday party, but he didn't invite you and you felt really bad. If you said to your mom, "I don't care—I didn't want to go to his old party anyway," would that be telling the truth? (No.) Do you think you would feel better if you said to your mom, "Mom, I wish I could go to the party. I feel so sad." And if maybe you even cried a little to get the sad out?

f. What if you forgot to wash your hands for lunch and your mother said, "Did you wash your hands?" If you said, "No, I forgot," would that be telling the truth? (Yes.)

g. What if you took a toy car from school, put it in your pocket, and took it home with you. Then when your mother saw you playing with it and asked, "Where did you get that little car?" if you said, "I brought it home from school," would you be telling the truth? (Yes.) But would it be all right to take home something that didn't belong to you? (No.)

10. Puppet shows on honesty. Each show will have two endings, a dishonest ending and an honest one.

a. Susie is four. Her brother, Robert, is six and goes to school. Susie and her brother each have a new puzzle. One day when Robert is at school, Susie wants to play with her puzzle but she can't find it. She thinks, "I'll play with Robert's. I'll be careful with the pieces and I'll put them back before he gets home." (Ask, "Do you think that was a good idea?")

It is a nice day, so Susie goes outside to play with the puzzle. She is having so much fun that she doesn't realize it is time for Robert to come home. She sees him coming along the sidewalk. She knows she shouldn't have taken the puzzle without asking, and she doesn't want him to see it, so she quickly closes the box and hides it under a bush.

Robert goes right to his room to get his puzzle to play with. When he can't find it, he says, "Susie, I can't find my puzzle. Do you know where it is?"

First ending: Susie says, "No, I haven't seen it." (Ask, "Did she tell the truth?") Susie thinks, "Tomorrow after Robert goes to school, I'll put his puzzle back in his room." But the next morning when she goes out to get it, the box isn't under the bush. She looks around and sees part of the box over by the fence. The wind must have blown it there. But almost all the pieces are gone. The wind has blown them all away. Because Susie has lost her brother's puzzle, Mother makes her give Robert her puzzle. (Ask, "How do you think she feels?")

Second ending: Susie says, "Yes, I took it because I couldn't find mine." She runs and gets it for him. Robert is angry, and he yells, "You leave my things alone," but pretty soon he gets over being angry. He helps Susie find her puzzle and they have fun playing together. (Ask, "How do you think Susie feels?")

b. Daddy asks Robert to go to the neighbor's house to borrow a screwdriver for him. The neighbors have a big black dog that always sits on their porch and barks at Robert whenever he goes by. Robert is afraid of that dog.

First ending: Robert says, "I don't want to go, Dad. My leg hurts." His leg doesn't really hurt, but he is afraid of the dog. The doorbell rings, and Father goes to the door. Robert can hear his friend asking if Robert can come out to play. His father says, "Robert's leg is hurting, so he won't be able to play today." (Ask, "How do you think Robert feels?")

Second ending: Robert says, "Please, Dad, I don't want to go." Father asks, "Why not?" and Robert says, "I'm afraid of their dog. He barks and growls at me." Father says, "I used to be afraid of him, too, until I got to know him. I'll go with you and help you get to know him." They go the neighbor's house. Father talks softly to the dog and calls him by name. The dog stops barking, wags his tail, and lets Robert pet him. (Ask, "How do you think Robert feels?")

c. Susie wants Mother to read her a story, but Mother doesn't have time right now because she is feeding the baby. It seems like Mother is always busy with the baby. Susie feels like she wishes they didn't even have a baby.

First ending: When Susie falls down, she cries even if it doesn't hurt, just so Mother will come to comfort her. Sometimes she says she is too tired to eat, just so Mother will feed her. Sometimes she knocks her milk on the floor just so Mother will have to put the baby down and come to clean it up. Mother gets angry and says, "Oh, Susie, you're acting like a baby." (Ask, "How do you think Susie feels?")

Second ending: Susie says, "Mommy, you're always taking care of the baby. I feel like you don't love me anymore. Why don't we give the baby away?" (Say, "That's how Susie really feels, and she tells her mother. Is it all right for Susie to say that?") Mother puts the baby in the crib, takes Susie on her lap, and gives her a big hug. She says, "I'm sorry, Susie. Babies do take lots of time. When you were a baby, I did all these things for you and I didn't have much time for Robert. I still love you just as much. You can help me give the baby his bath, and then I'll read you a story." (Ask, "How do you think Susie feels?")

III. Family Focal Point: Happys and Sads

Bedtime is a good time for a little honest, important dialogue between parent and child. Years ago we started a tradition of asking each child as he was tucked in, "What was your 'happy' and your 'sad' today?" Children like to think back through the day to recognize and talk about emotions. "My happy was when my friend came over to play," or "when I got two desserts," or "when I jumped in the leaf pile," or "when Daddy came home." "My sad was when Lisa wouldn't play with me at school," or "when I couldn't hop very well in hopscotch," or "when I cut my finger," or "I didn't have any sads today."

The answers open up quick, golden chances to talk about real feelings. "How did it feel to play with Susan?" "Why do you suppose Lisa wouldn't play? Did something sad happen to her?" "Did you feel that someone else was better at hopscotch than you?" "What can you do better than they?"

IV. Story: "Isabel's Little Lie"

One day Isabel told a little lie. She wasn't supposed to feed her dinner to her dog, Barker, but she did, and when her mother came in and saw her plate all clean, Isabel said that she had eaten it all. (That was a little lie, wasn't it?) The dinner was chicken, and Barker got a bone in his throat. Pretty soon he started to cough and snort and act very uncomfortable.

"Do you know what's wrong with Barker?" asked Mother. "No," said Isabel. (That was another lie, wasn't it? But Isabel *had* to do it so Mother wouldn't know she told the first lie.) Mother looked in Barker's mouth but couldn't see anything. "Did Barker eat something, Isabel?" "I don't know, Mommy." (That was another lie, wasn't it? But she didn't want her mother to know about the first two lies.)

Barker got worse, and Mother took him to the animal hospital. Isabel went too. "What happened to the dog?" asked the doctor. "We don't know," said Isabel. (That was another lie, wasn't it? But if Isabel had told, then Mother and the dog doctor would know she had lied before.) The dog doctor said, "If it's just a bone, we could get it out with an instrument, but it might be glass, so we may have to operate."

Isabel decided it was time to tell the truth. She said, "It's a bone, and I *did* know Barker ate it, and I *didn't* eat all my dinner, and I *did* give it to Barker, and I won't tell lies any more, because if you tell one you might have to tell more and more." Isabel started to cry, but her mother loved her, and she decided she really would tell the truth from then on.

V. Reading List (Including Out-of-print Titles)

Behrens, J. *How I Feel.* Chicago: Childrens Press, 1973. (Short, simple statements about such emotions as love, fear, pride, anger, joy, with photos of children.)

Berger, T. *I Have Feelings.* New York: Human Sciences Press, 1971. (How children feel in different situations.)

Brandenberg, F. *I Wish I Was Sick Too.* New York: Greenwillow Books, 1976. (About jealousy and how feelings change.)

Brown, M. W. *First Night Away from Home.* New York: Franklin Watts, 1960. (A child's feelings of insecurity.)

Cockett, M. *Look at the Little One.* Chicago: Childrens Press, 1976. (About jealousy.)

Crowe, R. *Clyde Monster.* New York: E. P. Dutton, 1976. (A little monster is afraid of the dark and people.)

Gackenbach, D. *Harry and the Terrible Whatzit.* Scholastic Book Services, 1977. (A child finds there was really nothing to be afraid of.)

Gross, A. *Sometimes I Worry.* Chicago: Childrens Press, 1978. (Imaginative text looks at worries with sensitivity and humor.)

Hanson, J. *I Don't Like Timmy.* Minneapolis: Carolrhoda Books, 1972. (Leads to discussion about jealousy.)

How Do You Feel? Chicago: Child's World, 1973. (Beautiful pictures that lead to discussions.)

Iverson, G. *I Want to Be Big.* New York: E. P. Dutton, 1979. (A child tells his conflicting emotions about growing up.)

Keats, E. J. *Peter's Chair.* New York: Harper and Row, 1957. (A little boy is jealous of a new baby.)

Sendak, M. *Where the Wild Things Are.* New York: Harper and Row, 1963. (A little boy handles his anger and frustration through imaginings and daydreaming.)

Tester, S. *Sometimes I'm Afraid.* Chicago: Child's World, 1979. (Explores the subject of children's fears.)

Whitney, A. *Just Awful.* Reading, Massachusetts: Addison-Wesley Publishing, 1971. (A little boy expriences many different feelings.)

Zolotow, C. *If It Weren't For You.* New York: Harper and Row, 1966. (A boy feels resentment towards his brother.)

Teaching
the
Joy of 12
Communication
and Relationships

There is, of course, a panacea, an absolute cure-all for human problems big and small. It is a thing called communication.

I. Examples and Description

A. *Adult:* I once knew a middle-aged man, an accountant, who had a ledger-book-sized Christmas-card list. In this thick book all the pages were filled; there were hundreds and hundreds of names. "Business contacts?" I asked. He glanced over, paused for a moment as though considering whether he should tell me something important, then said, "No, they're relationships." He anticipated my next question and went on in his accounting terminology: "Every relationship you form, no matter how small, if it is genuine, can be an asset of eternal duration. No other entry can cancel it out. Some of us spend all our time on temporary assets: money, positions, achievements. We ought to spend more on the eternal assets like relationships. Whenever I earn one, I make an entry on my Christmas card list."

I watched the accountant closer from then on and found that he practiced what he preached. When he met someone—on a plane, in his business, at a PTA meeting—his attitude seemed to be: "What can I learn from you? What is interesting and unique about you?" For him, life was a fascinating kaleidoscope of relationships, of endless people, each endlessly interesting and each offering more potential joy than a new car or a new position.

B. *Child:* For little children, particularly those with strong self-images, genuine relationships are easy. Friends came by the other night, a business acquaintance and his wife. The four of us sat in the parlor, playing self-conscious "I" games: "How can *I* impress them?" "What can we talk about that *I* know a lot about?" "How can *I* seem sophisticated and 'with it'?"

Meanwhile, their five-year-old daughter went upstairs to play with our daughter of the same age. Their discussion (I caught part of it when I went up to get some papers) was more mature than ours because it was real, honest, open, and without ulterior motives. "Janet, you should bring your pajamas next time you come. No one uses the bottom bunk bed, so we could sleep in the same room." "Will your mommy care if I do?" "No, she likes your mommy." "Good, because I like you." When it was time to go, they came downstairs holding hands, smiling, friends, as if they'd known each other for years.

II. Methods

A. *General ideas.*

1. Develop a tradition of listening. *Really* listen—use psychologist Karl Rogers's technique of not directing the conversation, but just acknowledging what children say and agreeing, letting them go on. Help children glimpse the joy of seeing the other person's point of view.

2. Have a sense of humor. Show how "crisis plus time usually equals humor." Laugh at your own mistakes, and laugh with children at every opportunity.

3. Always encourage children to hug and make up after a disagreement.

4. Show romantic love between parents: holding hands, kissing as you leave, opening the car door, sitting close together, avoiding harsh words, emphasizing loving words.

5. Teach and explain the Golden Rule.

6. Role reversal: let the children play parents and you play child, so they see and appreciate your problems.

7. Don't constantly tell children what to say while you are in public or they will not think of taking the initiative on their own. Don't say, "Say thank you" or "Say please" or "Tell him we must be going now." Talk to them *later* about what they should have said, and set the stage for them to speak appropriately and on their own next time.

B. *Communicate.*

1. Speak candidly, graphically, logically to children.

2. Help children write letters—you write what they express. Praise them for phrasing things well.

3. Give lavish praise whenever children explain or say anything particularly well.

4. At dinner, encourage a child to talk about something that he knows a lot about—perhaps something he has just learned and is proud to know.

5. Talk on the phone with children whenever possible.

6. Encourage children to take advantage of any speaking opportunities. Help them really communicate to an audience.

7. Try to avoid communicating *for* children—and don't give them a cue every time they are supposed to speak.

*8. Discuss the fact that people are the only ones who can communicate with words—they don't have to fight like animals. Say "Let's talk about it" whenever a conflict comes up.

C. *Relationships.*

1. Make their relationship with you a truly beautiful one.

*2. Talk out disagreements. Sit them down face to face to work out problems or disagreements they have with each other.

3. Be an example. Show that relationships should be more important than achievements by always taking time for a relationship (even when in the middle of an achievement).

4. Don't always step in on children's relationships or try to steer them too much—let them work things out. (My children were having a terrific fight in the back seat of our station wagon once when I had laryngitis. I found that they worked it out better on their own than they would have with my direction.)

*5. Role-play relationship problems and let the children give ways to solve particular difficulties. Role-play what to do if you want a toy someone else has, or if you hurt someone, or if you both want to be the mommy when you play house, or if someone calls you a bad name. Have children act out a situation that ended in unhappiness and show how it could have been handled better and ended happily.

6. Encourage children to have their own special friends over to play. (Sometimes this requires having other children play elsewhere for a while so that one child feels he has control of the situation.)

7. Do something special for your children to stress the importance of your friendship with them. Take them for a drive, or bring them a surprise.

8. Develop the family as a social unit. Encourage children to think of family members as their best friends. At first they may have to be told, as the following conversation illustrates:

Mother: "Josh, who's your best friend?"

Josh: "Christopher."

Mother: "But who is the friend you play with *most* of the time and the one who makes you laugh when she plays peek-a-boo?"

Josh: "Oh, Saydi."

Mother: "That's right."

9. Help children to identify and understand the feelings of others: "Why do you suppose she seems so unfriendly today? Maybe she doesn't feel well. Maybe someone was unfriendly to her."

*10. Make a little booklet of "kind words" with a child. Let him paste in the words:

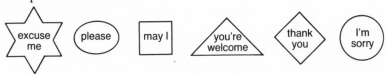

*11. Play the game "Which is the better way?" in which children act out a good and bad way of deciding who should have the first turn, getting the dishes done after Sunday dinner, getting ready for school in the morning, or deciding which television show to watch.

*12. Discuss how *talking* is the best way to communicate. Ask, "Animals can't talk with words, can they? How do *they* tell how they feel or what they want?"

—How does a dog tell you he likes you?

—How does a dog or a cat tell you he wants to go outside?

—How does a cat tell you he is happy?

—How does a cow tell the farmer she wants to be milked? (She "moos" loudly.)

—How does a rooster tell us it's morning, time to get up?

—When animals are angry with each other, do they stamp their feet and say, "I'm angry?" No. They bark or meow or growl. They bite and fight.

Conclude, "I'm glad I can talk. Are you glad you can talk? I'll talk to you and tell you something I want you to do, and if you know what my words mean, you do it."

Everyone stand up.

Turn around.

Touch your knees.

Scratch your back.

Rub your stomach.

Open your mouth.

Put your hands in the air.

Close your mouth.

Shake your arms.

Shake your legs.

Come over here (to a different area).
Sit back down.

III. Family Focal Point: "Guess Who's Coming to Dinner"

When Saren was four, she went through a short but painful phase of "I don't have any friends." She seemed shy in nursery school, not her normal, initiative-taking self. Then one day she asked if she could invite a friend over for dinner. Of course we were glad—a "breakthrough" perhaps? It was more than that. Something about having a friend in her home, to see her house and family, seemed to wipe the shyness away.

Ever since then, we have had one special supper every couple of weeks when one family member—on a rotating basis, parents included—has a friend over for the evening meal. It shows children how important relationships are, and it exposes them to strangers, to interesting people, some of whom are very different from them. It puts the premium where it should be: on the joy of communication and relationships.

IV. Story: "Herman Finds a Friend"

Herman was a baby bird. He had a mother who brought him worms to eat in their small nest in the big sycamore tree. He had learned to fly. He had pretty blue feathers. Nest, mother, worms, blue feathers, air to fly in—he had everything to make him happy, right?

Then why was Herman sad?

He didn't know why, but he was.

One day another bird's nest was built on the next highest limb of the tree. A new bird family, the Robin Redbreasts, moved in. They had a boy bird just Herman's age named Reginald. Herman and Reginald flew together, played together, explored together. Herman wasn't unhappy anymore.

What made the difference?

V. Reading List (Including Out-of-print Titles)

Anglund, J. Cowboy and His Friend. New York: Harcourt Brace Jovanovich, 1961. (A relationship with an imaginary friend.)

Behrens, J. *The Manners Book.* Chicago: Childrens Press, 1980. (How to deal with awkward situations.)

———. *Together.* Chicago: Childrens Press, 1975. (Best friends do all kinds of things together.)

Cohen, M. *Best Friends.* New York: Macmillan, 1973. (Relationships, good and bad, between friends.)

Dauer, R. *Bullfrog Builds a House.* New York: Greenwillow Books, 1977. (To enjoy his house, he needs someone to share it with.)

Delton, J. *Two Is Company.* New York: Crown Publishing, 1976. (Duck and bear learn from each other about relating to another animal in the forest.)

Ets. M. H. *Play With Me.* New York: Penguin Books, 1976. (A little girl makes friends with animals by being gentle.)

———. *Talking Without Words.* New York: Viking Press, 1968. (A special relationship between two friends.)

Flack, M. *Angus and the Cat.* New York: Doubleday, 1971. (A dog decides it is better not to be alone.)

Guilfoile, E. *Nobody Listens to Andrew.* New York: Scholastic Book Services, 1973. (It's important to *listen* as well as to talk.)

Gurney, N. and E. *The King, the Mice and the Cheese.* New York: Penguin Books, 1965. (By communicating and discussing disagreements we can learn to get along with each other.)

Hallinan, P. K. *That's What a Friend Is.* Chicago: Childrens Press, 1977. (Describes the aspects of a close friendship.)

Heine, H. *Friends.* New York: Atheneum, 1982.

Hutchins, P. *Rosie's Walk.* New York: Macmillan, 1968. (A story with few words but a lot to talk about.)

Joslin, S. *What Do You Say, Dear?* New York: Scholastic Book Services, 1980. (A silly book of manners for all occasions.)

Lobel, A. *Frog and Toad Are Friends.* New York: Harper and Row, 1979.

———. *Frog and Toad Together.* New York: Harper and Row, 1979.

Marshall, J. *George and Martha.* Boston: Houghton Mifflin, 1974.

McPhail, D. *Alligators Are Awful, and They Have Terrible Manners, Too.* New York: Doubleday, 1980. (About being rude to others.)

Moncure, J. *Caring.* Chicago: Childrens Press, 1981. (Ways to help and show sympathy and empathy.)

————. *I Never Say I'm Thankful, But I Am.* Chicago: Child's World, 1979. (A child's expressions of gratitude—beautiful illustrations.)

————. *Love.* Chicago: Childrens Press, 1981. (Ways to demonstrate love for others.)

Polushkin, M. *Mother, Mother I Want Another.* New York: Scholastic Book Services, 1980. (Misunderstanding what someone says can cause lots of trouble.)

Riley, S. *What Does It Mean? Sorry.* Chicago: Childrens Press, 1978.

Slobodkin, L. *One Is Good But Two Are Better.* New York: Vanguard Press, 1956. (Many pleasant experiences need to be shared with someone.)

Smaridge, N. *Raggedy Ann—A Thank You, Please, and I Love You Book.* New York: Golden Press, 1970. (About kindness, consideration, and good manners.)

Udry, J. *Let's Be Enemies.* New York: Harper and Row, 1961. (Even best friends don't always get along.)

Williams, B. *Albert's Toothache.* New York: E. P. Dutton, 1974. (We need to understand what someone means . . . not just listen to what he says.)

Zolotow, C. *Big Sister, Little Sister.* New York: Harper and Row, 1966. (The relationship between two sisters.)

————. *Do You Know What I'll Do?* New York: Harper and Row, 1958. (A sweet relationship and show of love.)

————. *My Friend John.* New York: Harper and Row, 1968. (A special relationship between two friends.)

————. *The Quarreling Book.* New York: Harper and Row, 1963. (Shows how feelings and actions are contagious.)

Teaching the Joy of Sharing and Service

13

The only ones around you who will be really happy are those who will have sought and found how to serve. (Albert Schweitzer.)

I. Examples and Description

A. *Adult:* I have a friend who taught me a lesson about joy. He is a public person: that is, the public knows him. (I would guess that 50 percent of all persons in the western world recognize his name, 95 percent of those interested in sports.) One of our conversations was about pleasure. What did we do with our spare time? What did we do with those rare moments— rarer for him than for me—that we really had to ourselves? (Keep in mind, he could do anything, go anywhere, have anything that money could buy.) He said, "When I have a moment for myself, I try to use it to find some way to help someone. That's where I find real happiness. It's so much more fun than doing something for yourself."

I'd heard that you can judge a man by what he does with his spare time. I used that criteria and judged this man to be great; maybe more importantly, I judged him to be joyful, because the joy of giving is so deep. The joy comes from losing one's self in helping others, from dismissing self-worries to make room for other-worries. We make our living by what we get, but we make our life by what we give. Emerson said, "See how the masses of men worry themselves into nameless graves . . . while, here and there, a great, unselfish soul forgets himself into immortality."

I was traveling on business, two full days away, meetings all day, free evenings. The first night I treated myself (hard day, I deserved it) to the finest meal at the finest restaurant. I went to bed satisfied, dulled. The next evening on my way to the same spot, I noticed a blind man sitting with his dog in front of a little shop, selling baskets he had made. I stopped, talked for an hour, bought a basket and a stool, cheered him up, listened to him, learned from him. ("I've lost one sense and gained four," he said.) I told him that I liked his company, liked him as a friend, and that I'd be back. I saw tears in his blind eyes as we shook hands. I went to bed that night thrilled, tingling— and, in a small but deep sort of way, a better man.

B. *Child:* On the Christmas when Saren was four and Shawni was three, we tried something. Starting in the fall, they began to "earn" their own money by doing extra household chores. Each got a new piggy bank "for deposit only." I was amazed at the anticipation of a three-year-old and how anxious she was to "buy my own presents for people with my own 'earned money.'"

That year, there were two Christmas days. One was on the twenty-third of December when we went to the variety store and the girls picked out a teacup for Grandma, measuring spoons for Mommy, and a tennis ball for two-year-old Josh (because "he can start thinking about how to hit it"). They watched the check-out clerk count their nickels and pennies. They carried their carefully concealed treasures up to their rooms and wrapped them themselves. All the while they were anticipating the joy of giving, sharing, making others happy; the feelings grew and became real from within. "Won't Grandpa be happy when he sees this?" "What will Mommy say when she opens this?"

When Christmas day came, the reactions were remarkable. The children were still grateful for their own dolls and filled stockings, but we saw real joy in the four-year-old's face when Grandma opened her cup and said, "Oh, Saren, just what I needed. Every time I use it, I'll think of you." There was a tear in the four-year-old's eye and a choke of real joy in her voice when Saren said, "I saved up and picked it out for you, Grandma, because I love you." Since then, we've thought back countless times: "Wasn't it fun when Josh opened his ball? Didn't that make us happy?" Children can feel the joy of sharing and service, and when they feel it, they want it again—and when they want it again, they've learned it.

We took a group of children to an old folks' home to put on a program, to pass out little gifts they had made, and to share their love. We explained, "These are old people without grandchildren to love them." I wish I had a picture of one three-year-old on an eighty-year-old's knee, arms around the neck, tears in all four eyes. And the joy of reflection afterward, as one four-year-old said to another, "We made the grandpas and grandmas happy, didn't we?" "Yes, and they made me happy." "Let's do it again."

A personal recollection (Linda's) may further illustrate the joy:

I remember that a particularly miserable time in my life came when I was in the sixth grade. I was eleven years old, considered my leftover baby fat anything but cute, and wore salmon-colored "cat-eye" glasses which I abhorred. I sensed that I had no style and, worst of all, thought I had no friends. I was worried about who liked me and who didn't, and each day I wondered whether or not the one marginal friend I thought I had would be nice to me.

One Saturday afternoon while I was getting ready for a school party, I began telling my mother my feelings. I don't remember whether I just had not bothered to tell them to her before or whether she had passed them off lightly as childish whims when I had mentioned them. On this particular day, however, she took me seriously and could see that I was really concerned. As I donned my party clothes, I said, "Mom, sometimes I feel so left out when I'm with other people. I just can't think of anything to say and yet I feel so uncomfortable if no one talks to me."

My mom, in her wisdom, gave me some counsel in those next few minutes that changed my life: "Linda, whenever you are with a group of people who are socializing with one another, look around; just stand back and look around a few minutes, and you will almost always see someone who needs you, someone who is feeling insecure and in need of a friend. You can tell by a look in the eye, a nervous mannerism, someone off by herself. Decide who needs *you* and then go to *them;* relate to them, ask questions about them, show them you care!"

This advice was like a miracle drug for my ailing soul. I went to the party. I stood back and observed. "There she is," I thought as I saw Beverly, the girl with the stringy hair and the buckteeth, sweet but not too bright. Everyone knew that she lived in a strange, broken-down house outside of town with about nine brothers and sisters, equally untidy and shabby. I remember her as though it were yesterday, sitting quietly in a chair, looking at her hands, while those around her giggled and chattered and ignored her. *But what will everyone think?* I cringed in my immature mind. *If I talk to her, everyone will think I'm dumb and "out of it" like she is.* But my conscience told me it was right, so I walked over to her. Suddenly, instead of muddling in my own misery because I didn't have any friends, I became *her* friend. I started by asking questions about her family and farm, and as the party wore on, I felt her warm acceptance and saw the joy in her eyes as she understood that somebody cared about her. But even more important to me, *I* was needed. I was providing a service to someone that, in time, made me grow to appreciate her. I also noticed that no one shunned me because of my association with her.

The experience gave me such a good feeling that I tried to pick out those who needed someone in other situations. As I began to forget myself in other people, I found that I was surrounded by a host of friends who really liked me for what I was.

If I could instill this in our children at an even younger age, how great their rewards would be. So often we say, "Oh, they're too young to understand." I wonder. Try teaching this principle to a four-year-old—you might be surprised.

II. Methods.

A. *By example.* Oh, how children learn by what their parents do! Help an old woman with her bags. Take any opportunity to help someone while your children are with you. Build a family reputation for service and for helping. Always stop to help people in distress, people out of gas, people looking for directions. Let your children see that helping other people is the thing to do.

B. *Help the less fortunate.*

1. Sponsor a child. There are many "sponsoring" organizations that give opportunities at a moderate cost to feel the joy of sharing with others who are in real need. Let your children miss a meal once a month and send the money to a sponsored child; the organization will send pictures and letters of appreciation from the child. The joy of gratitude can intermingle here with the joy of service.

2. Help children who don't have strong families. Perhaps an orphan's home nearby allows children to go on picnics with families. Is there a neighbor child who doesn't have a happy family life? Could you include him in your family activity? Let the children feel the happiness of giving happiness.

3. Story: "Alice Learns about Sharing."

Late in December, a new girl came to Alice's class. She was smaller than Alice and kind of thin, but pretty, with large, brown eyes and dark hair. Her dress was too big for her, and, though it was clean, it looked old and worn. Her name was Heather. She sat right next to Alice. The two girls quickly became friends, and after school Heather asked Alice if she could come to her house to play. They stopped first at Alice's house to ask her mother and then went on to Heather's house.

Alice noticed as they walked along that Heather didn't have any boots or gloves and that her coat was thin; she looked like she was cold. She held her coat tightly around her because the zipper was broken.

Heather lived in a small, gray house across the railroad tracks. The porch railing was broken and the paint was peeling off. She lived with her grandmother, who was quite old and who looked tired and worried.

Alice said, "Let's play house. What kind of dolls do you have?"

Heather said, "I have only this one doll, but you can use it and you can be the mommy." It was a small rag doll with only one arm and no clothes. Heather said, "I asked my grandmother if I could have a new doll for my birthday, but she said she didn't even have enough money for food, and she couldn't buy a doll."

Alice noticed that Heather didn't have many other toys and that there was only one other dress in her closet. She also noticed that the house was not very warm and that the furniture was old and the curtains were torn.

But Heather was fun to play with, and her grandma was nice.

Soon it was time for Alice to go. She said good-bye to Heather and hurried home.

She told her mother all about her new friend and about her cold house and her old doll and her thin coat and that she had no boots or gloves and didn't even have a mother or father. She liked Heather a lot, and she kept thinking about her.

Then she had an idea. "Mother, Heather's birthday is Saturday. I want to give her one of my dolls. She could have Susie—she's still as good as new. And she could have my blue coat. It's too small for me, but it would fit her. And Mother, you know that money I was saving for a bicycle? I can't ride a bike in the winter anyway. I could buy some boots and gloves for Heather. Maybe I could give her one of my dresses, too, if you could shorten it a little. I think she would look nice in the yellow one with the little flowers on it."

Her mother said, "Alice, I think that's a wonderful idea.

We could wrap all the things up and leave them on Heather's porch. I think we should put in a gift for Heather's grandmother, too." Then Mother added, "Would you like to invite them to have dinner with us?"

"Oh, yes," answered Alice. "And let's not tell who the presents are from."

For the next few days, Alice and her mother shopped for boots and gloves and wrapped gifts. On Friday, after dark, they went to Heather's house. They quietly set the presents on the porch, knocked on the door, and then hurried away.

(Pause while the children experience the joy of imagining what happened next.)

When Heather and her grandmother came to Alice's house for dinner the next day, Heather was wearing a warm blue coat and new boots and gloves and holding a beautiful doll tightly in her arms. She said, "Oh, Alice, just see what I got for my birthday—and Grandma got a new sweater." Then Heather took off her coat, and under it she wore a pretty yellow dress with flowers on it.

Alice smiled and smiled. She felt so happy that she could hardly speak. "Oh, Heather," she exclaimed, "I'm glad you had such a lovely birthday."

C. *Serving each other within the family.*

1. Perform "services" for each other. Services include anything from helping brother find his socks to letting sister use the new crayons. If we want children to love, we must teach them to serve. Older children can serve their younger brothers and sisters in countless ways.

2. Let children serve you. Make little comments like, "Oh, the paper is on the porch and I am so tired." "I can't pull these boots off." "I can't hold this leaf bag open while I dump the leaves in." "My arms are full; now how am I going to get in this door?" It's better when they volunteer to help than when you ask them directly.

D. *Doing good deeds together.*

*1. Help a needy family anonymously. Have each child sacrifice a toy.

2. Do "secret good turns." Watch for people in need, and plan for ways to make them happier. Have discussions with the children on how what you have done will make other people happy. Children can pretend to be good little elves (in-

visible, of course) who clean up the house or do other good turns. Mother will "wonder" who could have done it.

3. Service project. Prearrange with a neighbor to rake her leaves or make a snowman in her front yard. If the weather is just too miserable, make a small cake or premixed cookies and take them to someone who would appreciate them. Inform the "targets" that you are coming and encourage them to show lavish appreciation to the children for their service.

E. *Sharing games.*

*1. Feeding each other: at lunchtime, tie splints to children's arms so they can't bend their elbows. Ask, "How are you going to eat?" (They will have to feed each other.)

*2. Sharing tools: Pass out modeling clay but give each child only one tool (one a roller, one a cookie cutter, etc.). Ask, "How can you make everything you want with only one tool?" (They can share tools.)

III. Family Focal Point: The Family Round Table

We have a big round table in the family room. Whenever a family member finds something worth sharing—a special picture, a pretty rock, a new book, anything he wants to pass around—it is put on the round table. Children, aware of that table and the opportunity they have to put something on it, seem to become more oriented not only to sharing but also to observing, to finding something worthwhile to share. It needn't be a round table; it could be any place designated for the joy of sharing.

IV. Story: "The Sharing Tree"

"Please don't make me push them any further," little Oakley pleaded. "It's so cold and damp down there, and I keep bumping into rocks." The baby oak tree was about to cry when Oakhurst, the grand old oak standing beside him, explained again, "Now, Oakley, my son, soon it will be spring, with hard spring winds, and then summer, with summer storms. Your roots must be strong to hold the rest of you in place. They must be deep in the rich, moist soil to find nourishing food to make your trunk and branches sturdy and healthy. By next year you will have grown so much, you won't believe it!" "Very well," sighed Oakley with a sad but determined grunt. He pushed his roots deeper into the ground, a little further each day, until spring arrived.

One warm, beautiful spring day, Oakley glanced over at his branches and was amazed to see beautiful green buds all over his tips. He thought they were gorgeous, and he was feeling great until one day he started to feel that his beautiful buds were about to burst. "Oh, Oakhurst," he gasped as he looked at his magnificent friend beside him, "my branches, my beautiful branches! They're about to burst, and I can't stop them, no matter how hard I try!" "My dear Oakley," smiled the big, calm tree, "stop trying! Instead of losing something, you'll find a pleasant surprise. You must learn that when you let go of something precious to you, it will be replaced by something better." Because he trusted his kind friend so much, Oakley reluctantly let go. Almost like hundreds of little jack-in-the-boxes, tiny green leaves began to appear all over his branches. "Oh, look at me now!" Oakley cried. "You were right!"

As days passed, Oakley became more and more beautiful. He loved the feeling of the wind rustling through his leaves, but the thing that made him happiest was to watch the lovely family of robins who had built their home in his branches. They were happy there, and that made Oakley happy too. He was so glad that he was strong and sturdy with deep roots and that he was sharing with others the beauty and comfort of his leaves. Before long he noticed little brown seeds beginning to form, which Oakhurst told him were acorns; he was proud of them, too.

One day as he was watching the robin children play, he noticed that his leaves were not so green. Some had even begun to turn gold, and one of his acorns fell off, and then another, and then another and another. "Stop!" he screamed. "I need you all to keep me beautiful!" But they continued to fall, and he shouted, "Oakhurst, what is happening? I'm changing color, and my acorns are falling!" "Don't be afraid," said Oakhurst kindly. "Remember what I said to you before. Any time you give up something special to you, you are giving service, and it will be replaced by something better. Soon you will lose all your acorns. Many of them will be gathered up by our little friends the squirrels, who will store them for food for the winter so they won't be hungry when all the berries have gone. Some will even find a warm spot in the earth, and then when spring comes, they will sprout roots of their own and begin to grow. And you'll find that you'll turn from green to gorgeous orange and red, and then the weather will turn cold

and you'll lose all your leaves." "Lose all my leaves!" shrieked
Oakley. "Then I will be ugly and cold, and I'll never grow to be
so wise and beautiful as *you*." "Ah, you are wrong, my little
friend," said the grand old Oakhurst. "That's exactly how I became wise and strong."

At the time, Oakley thought that was all very strange, but
as the days passed he began to realize what his friend meant.
He saw his acorns drop and his little friends gather them for
winter food. His leaves turned a beautiful red, and then, just
as Oakhurst had said, they began to drop off. He was sad at
first, but when he saw the children rustling through them and
having so much fun playing in them, he was glad for the opportunity to share. And when the cold winter came (and Oakley did look a bit ugly some days) he was happy that he had
shared himself. He knew that when springtime came again he
would be stronger, his roots would be longer, his leaves and
branches would be bigger, and he would be better . . . and
more like his great friend Oakhurst.

V. Reading List (Including Out-of-print Titles)

Bannon, L. *The Gift of Hawaii*. Chicago: Albert Whitman,
1961. (A child searches for a special gift for mother.)

Bonsall, C. *It's Mine*. New York: Harper and Row, 1964.
(About selfishness and the consequences.)

Brown, M. *Benjy's Blanket*. New York: Franklin Watts, 1962.
(Benjy shares his precious possession with one who needs
it.)

Duvoisen, R. *Veronica*. New York: Alfred Knopf, 1961. (You
learn to love someone when you help and share.)

Flack, M. *Ask Mister Bear*. New York: Macmillan, 1971. (A
child finds the best gift for mother.)

Galdone, P. *The Little Red Hen*. Boston: Houghton Mifflin,
1973. (In this version the animals learn to help.)

Heide, F. *That's What Friends Are For*. New York: Scholastic
Books, 1971. (Friends learn that giving advice is not the
same as helping.)

Holl, A. *The Poky Little Puppy's First Christmas*. New York: Gold-
en Press, 1973. (Puppy learns to care about and share with
others.)

———. *We Help Daddy*. New York: Golden Press, 1979. (Ways
child can help father.)

Karr, D. *Cookie Monster and the Cookie Tree.* New York: Golden Press, 1977. (Cookie Monster learns to share.)

Kraus, R. *Herman the Helper.* New York: Windmill Books, 1974.

Moncure, J. *Kindness.* Chicago: Childrens Press, 1980. (Examples of children sharing and serving.)

———. *The Shoemaker and the Christmas Elves.* Child's World, 1980. (The elves give and receive service and joy.)

Odor, R. *A Friend Is One Who Helps.* Chicago: Child's World, 1979. (Several people pass Sara by, but one friend stops to help.)

Peet, B. *The Ant and the Elephant.* Boston: Houghton Mifflin, 1972. (Helping someone else often yields help in return.)

Riley, S. *What Does It Mean? Help.* Chicago: Child's World, 1978. (Children can help and be helped. Helping makes us feel good.)

———. *What Does It Mean? Sharing.* Chicago: Childrens Press, 1978.

Silverstein, S. *The Giving Tree.* New York: Harper and Row, 1964. (A tree finds happiness through giving all it has to a friend.)

Williams, B. *Jeremy Isn't Hungry Anymore.* New York: E. P. Dutton, 1978.

Wing, H. *Ten Pennies for Candy.* New York: Holt, Rinehart and Winston, 1963. (A child finds joy in sharing with friends.)

Winthrop, E. *That's Mine.* New York: Holiday House, 1977. (Two children learn to share and co-operate.)

Postscript: Setting Up
a Neighborhood "Joy School"

Many parents will be satisfied to use the idea and methods of this book in their own households. Others will want a way to involve their children in a Joy School where they can learn many of the joys in a group setting with their peers. This section is for those of you in that second category.

Let us once again be a little personal and tell you the origin of the Joy School idea. When we completed the writing of the first edition of *Teaching Children Joy* in 1980, we thought we were finished. As it turned out, we were just getting started!

We had included in that original edition, as in this one, a suggestion for cooperative neighborhood Joy Schools where mothers would rotate as teachers and use our book as a curriculum, working on one kind of joy each month.

No sooner had the book been published than we started getting cards, letters, and even phone calls. This was unusual; we had written other books but had never had so much response. It's a lot of trouble to get an author's address and phone number, but people were taking the trouble to contact us, and their comments were not all complimentary.

As a matter of fact, virtually all the comments were focusing on one thing: the suggestion we had made about do-it-yourself Joy Schools. One call, from a woman who did not identify herself, typified all the responses but in a slightly more blunt and direct manner. I've often wished I could locate the woman, because she is probably responsible for the TCJ parent group program, which now has tens of thousands of members.

I happened to be home alone when the call came. I said, "Hello." And she demanded, without any hesitation and in a somewhat hostile voice, "Are you the one who wrote this book on teaching children joy?"

My natural cowardice showed as I answered, "Well, actually it was mostly my wife who wrote it."

She said, "Is she there?"

I said, "No, she is out."

She was undeterred. "Well, then, I'll just have to talk to you, won't I, Mr. Eyre?"

I said, "I suppose you will." They were the last words I had a chance to say for some time.

Then she unloaded. "Mr. Eyre, I have some good news for you and some bad news."

(I hoped for the good news first and I got it.)

"I love your book! I have two little preschoolers, and our neighborhood is full of young families. I've been looking for ways to give them self-esteem and social happiness, and your book is *perfect*. And it's practical because it gives me workable methods to teach my children how to be happy!"

(Well, I thought, this isn't so bad after all.) I tried to thank her but she was already into her next section.

"Now for the bad news! The bad news is that you led me down the garden path! You suggested on page eleven that we start a neighborhood preschool group, teach it ourselves, and use your book as a curriculum to teach joy. Well, I took you at your word. I got six mothers together, and we decided to have a Joy School two mornings per week. I volunteered to teach first and picked 'The Joy of Obedience and Decisions' as the first unit."

(Her voice was getting higher and higher. I felt grateful that this was a phone call rather than a personal meeting.)

"I got those six little three-year-olds in my living room. I told them the two stories from that chapter in your book. I did the finger play and sang the song with them and did every other method in the chapter, and it all went fine, just fine. But do you know how long it all *took*, Mr. Eyre?"

(She didn't wait for an answer.)

"It took thirteen minutes! And I still had two and a half *hours* before the mothers came back to get their kids. They nearly killed me! They nearly killed each other! I think if you are going to suggest Joy Schools with inexperienced mothers trying to teach, you ought to give us a real curriculum!"

(I started to say something like "thank you for your suggestions," but she had only paused for breath.)

"Well, that's what I have to say, Mr. Eyre. There are a lot of us out here who can't afford commercial preschools or who don't want them because we want to teach our own kids. And you got our hopes up because we agree with your philosophy about joy. But I think if you're going to suggest real schools, you need to tell us how to get real curriculums! Good-bye!"

If it had been an isolated call, we could have gotten over it. The problem was that it was the same message (albeit in stronger language) that the other calls and letters contained.

We were realizing how many families are caught in the dilemma of wanting a peer group experience for their small children but, for whatever reasons, not wanting a commercial preschool. We were also realizing how many of these parents liked the idea of teaching their children joy rather than some more academic option.

Neighborhood play groups or nurseries were not a new idea. They existed all over, with mothers taking turns watching each other's children. Mothers do this not only to give their children a social experience but to give *themselves* more free time. We found, however, that these neighborhood co-ops always fit one of two patterns. Either they were just babysitting, with no real effort to teach the children anything, or they were real efforts at preschool, with mothers spending ten to fifteen hours to prepare a three-hour lesson. We found that mothers wanted to teach more in these groups but didn't have the ability or the time to prepare elaborate lesson plans.

To make a long story short, we decided to do something about it. By then, our one commercial Joy School (which had been the basis for most of the ideas in this book) had been operating for six years and had developed extensive lesson plans and teaching materials. We (and the teachers at the school) rewrote these lesson plans in careful detail and made them available to mothers who wanted to use them in neighborhood co-ops.

Because the lesson plans were so detailed and complete (that is, at 9:30 tell this story, at 9:35 teach this song, at 9:40 . . .) mothers who used them gained confidence. They began to realize that if they had good materials they could be good teachers.

Each chapter in this book expanded into a 200-page monthly lesson manual for one type of joy, complete with pictures, music, puppet patterns, and everything else a mother would need to cut down her preparation time and give her confidence as a teacher. People wanted the manuals so badly that we soon had several thousand families involved and had developed "economies of scale" to the point where we could add a newsletter and an audio tape to the monthly manual and still make it available to families for only a few dollars. Unlike this book, where methods and ideas can only be described, the TCJ manuals and tapes can teach through songs and music, through art materials and projects, and through a whole range of teaching aids that are included in the lesson plan supplements. Special songbooks and illustrated children's storybooks on various "joys" are also provided.

Today, TCJ groups exist in almost every part of the country. Typically, one family gets started in the program and then adds others until there are three to six parents rotating as teacher. The parents meet together early each month to get their materials from the group leader and to decide which parent will teach each week during the month ahead. The meeting makes parents more aware of what they are trying to teach and more committed to it. Each Joy School day, the children bring home a note reviewing what they've been learning so that parents can reinforce it in the home. The newsletter stays in each home during the month to provide additional ideas and suggestions for parents on the same "joy" the children are learning in joy school.

A year or so after the first neighborhood Joy Schools started, we received a letter that we thought summarized the benefits and advantages of TCJ. The letter was from a Joy School mother and went something like this:

"We had thought of sending our child to a preschool for two reasons:

"1. To teach him something,

"2. To give me a little free time.

"The problem was that we weren't sure we could afford it and we weren't quite sure we liked everything it taught or that we wanted to give up the idea of teaching our little boy ourselves. Then TCJ came along and we got involved. It accomplishes the two things we had listed *plus* a whole set of other things that a commercial preschool could never do. Here's what I think TCJ does:

"1. Not only teaches the children 'something' but teaches them the capacities for happiness—teaches them actual *joy*.

"2. Frees the time of the mothers (except the mother actually teaching the group).

"3. Teaches the *mothers* the skills of preschool education and involves them firsthand in observing the learning and progress of the children.

"4. Involves the *fathers* as they read the monthly newsletter and stay abreast of what the children are learning each day they go to 'group.'

"5. Gives children the security-enhancing experience of being in their friends' houses and having personal relationships with their friends' mothers (and of having their friends in *their* home).

"6. Brings mothers together in a sharing, helping environment where they work together in helping each other and giving feedback to each other about one another's children.

"7. 'Popularizes' parenting. Causes parents to talk more about parenting, to think more about it, to be more aware of it, and thus to get better at it.

"8. Saves us money (it's a tenth the cost of preschool)."

A little later, we received another letter that gave a rather different perspective of TCJ. It was from a mother who had been working full time and had shifted to part-time work in order to be more involved with her three-year-old and with TCJ. She said:

"I had two reasons for working full time. One was that we needed a second income. The other was that I felt I needed the other things my job gave me: a chance to work with other adults, to use my full abilities and potential, and to work on *objectives* or projects where we could see our progress and get recognition and fulfillment.

"TCJ gives me these very things that I thought I could get only from my job. I work with the other mothers in our group . . . in a very organized and challenging program . . . we have objectives each month and can see the results. And the results we see are in our children!

"TCJ makes parenting pleasurable because it *organizes* it. It also brings us *together* as parents where we can share and

brainstorm. Most of all, it makes parenting pleasurable because we *succeed* with our children."

TCJ is now a national parents co-op involving tens of
thousands of preschoolers and their families. Each year the
methods and lesson plans improve because of the feedback
from TCJ members who repeat the program each year that
they have preschoolers. Each year, each child absorbs more
because he is a year older, and each parent teaches better because he or she has an additional year's experience.

The truth is that most parents, including ourselves, need
more than theories, more than books full of good ideas and
techniques. We need a program that regularly brings us together with other parents and gives us objectives, incentives,
and a "track to run on." This is what TCJ attempts to do.
For further information, write to TCJ, Lamplighter Square,
1615 Foothill Drive, Salt Lake City, Utah 84108, or call (801)
581-0112.

Index

Linda and Richard Eyre are at the forefront of a national trend toward more involved, more committed parenting.

Linda Eyre, Utah's 1981 Young Mother of the Year, was named by the National Council of Women as one of America's six outstanding young women. She is an accomplished violinist, author of three books, and mother of eight children. She holds a degree in music from Utah State University.

Richard Eyre was appointed by President Reagan as National Chairman of the 1981 White House Conference on Parents and Children. In 1982 he was appointed a member of the President's Advisory Panel on Financing Elementary and Secondary Education. President of a management consulting firm based in Washington, D.C., and Salt Lake City, Mr. Eyre holds degrees from Utah State, Brigham Young, and Harvard universities. He is the author of thirteen books.

The Eyres' books *Teaching Children Joy* and *Teaching Children Responsibility* have spawned two organizations called TCJ and TCR. These involve tens of thousands of parents who conduct do-it-yourself preschools in their own homes, following the Eyres' curriculum to supplement the education of their elementary-school-age children.

TCJ/TCR
Lamplighter Square
1615 Foothill Drive
Salt Lake City, Utah 84108

. . . .

Please send:
- ☐ 1. Additional information on TCJ (monthly lesson manuals, tapes, and newsletters for do-it-yourself, in-home "joy schools" for three- and four-year-olds, where mothers rotate as teachers).
- ☐ 2. Additional information on TCR (a monthly curriculum guide for "dinnertime sessions" where parents teach a form of responsibility each month and supplement the academics of public elementary schools).